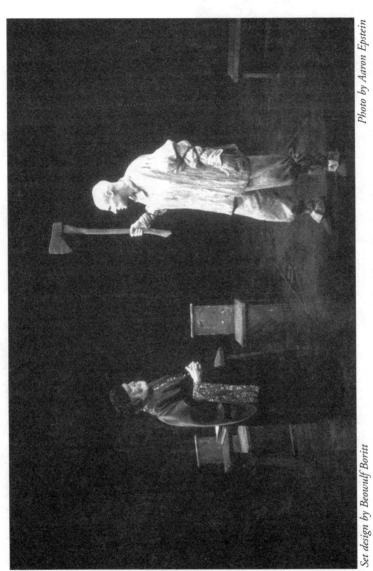

Set design by *Beowulf Boritt*

Photo by Aaron Epstein

A scene from the Manhattan Ensemble Theatre's production of *The Golem*.

THE GOLEM

BY H. LEIVICK

ADAPTED BY
DAVID FISHELSON

FROM A TRANSLATION BY
JOSEPH C. LANDIS

★

★

DRAMATISTS
PLAY SERVICE
INC.

THE GOLEM
Copyright © 2001, Manhattan Ensemble Theater, Inc.

All Rights Reserved

SPECIAL NOTE

THE GOLEM
by H. Leivick
Adapted by David Fishelson
from a Translation by Joseph C. Landis

THE GOLEM AND INNOCENCE LOST

> *I can forgive Israel's enemies many things,*
> *but not for turning its children into soldiers.*
> —Golda Meir

In the context of the ongoing Mideast crisis, one might be tempted to see *The Golem* as somehow advocating Jewish pacifism — or even *passivity* — in the face of destruction. "Are we thus chastised because we wished to protect ourselves, O Lord?" agonizes the Maharal during the play's tragic climax.

In the play, the Jews of Prague in 1580 face persecution. When they try to arm themselves by creating a Golem, horrible consequences ensue. A theatergoer's instinct might be to draw an analogy to recent Jewish history: In the wake of the Holocaust, the Jews of the world "armed" themselves by creating the state of Israel (a "Golem") to stay further genocide. But now, they — like the Jews of Prague — find themselves caught in a cycle of violence that appears to have no end: They must endure the ongoing anguish that comes from fighting fire with fire. As Reb Bassevi says in Scene 3 of *The Golem*: "Won't those who lift the sword fare worse? In doing so won't they lose their share of the world to come?" To which the Maharal replies: "Whether in this world or the next: There may be no tomorrow for Jews who meekly lay their necks upon the block."

The richness of *The Golem* — indeed, the play's courage, I think — is that it unblinkingly confronts this central, tragic aspect of the Jewish experience since the Diaspora. The horrid necessity of having to "lift the sword" is echoed in Golda Meir's quote above. Innocence has been lost. But the alternative (allowing another Holocaust) is unthinkable.

Like any tragedy, *The Golem* dramatizes the feelings behind this loss of innocence. The play, I would argue, is the pacifist dream of a Jewish poet — written 20 years before Auschwitz — *who dreads the impending, permanent loss of his people's innocence. The Golem is*

3

not, in this light, a denial of the necessity of resorting to violence. It is the lament of its necessity on this earth.

Americans after 9/11 (and especially New Yorkers) suffer from a similar loss of innocence. A people attacked is forced to become something other than what it was. We feel terror first; then numbness; and finally anger, bitterness and the desire to lash out in retaliation. Only the most committed pacifists believe such retaliation is not an option. Only the most hardened hearts feel joy at having been thus transformed.

In *The Golem*, it is finally the hardness of the Maharal's heart — more than his having resorted to war — that must be seen as his tragic flaw. The Maharal has become a warrior, yes, and certainly by necessity. But he's allowed this transformation to "take away the light that was his ... the gleaming light and radiant glow of our common trust and faith" [*The Golem,* Scene 3]. Had this warrior clung fast to the ideals of love and faith that were his before the terror — had he been kinder to the Golem, had he been ruled by love instead of hate *even as he went to war* — then perhaps his tragic fate could have been averted. "Who will save us?" goes the refrain that echoes throughout the play. The answer may well be: only ourselves — our better nature, and the love of life with which all of us were born.

* * *

H. Leivick originally wrote *The Golem* (first published in 1921) to be read, not performed. Though it *has* been produced frequently throughout the world since its premiere in Moscow in 1925, the play has always been trimmed for performance. The Manhattan Ensemble Theater adaptation you'll read is but the latest in a series of adaptations that have been visited on the work.

This particular adaptation was born of a conversation I had in the summer of 2001 with Prof. Joseph C. Landis, the translator (in 1966) of a famous volume called *Five Great Jewish Plays* (later *Three Great Jewish Plays* in its 1970s and 1980s reprints). Prof. Landis

4

encouraged me to do a new adaptation that would make the play newly accessible to today's theater audiences. With his encouragement and editorial advice, I worked from his translation.

The main work of my adaptation has been to heighten the plot's movement. What Landis has called the "arias" or long speeches of the play have been trimmed to their essence. The language has been tweaked slightly in an attempt to give the dialogue an immediacy — always taking care to preserve the power of the original verse. Scenes that diverged completely from the central plot were cut (notably much of Scene 7 in the original), and the arc of the play's latter half has been tightened. But taken as a whole, the play you'll see tonight is, in every way, H. Leivick's *The Golem*: with a new coat of paint on it, perhaps, but delivered intact.

—David Fishelson
New York City
April 2002

THE GOLEM was originally produced by the Manhattan Ensemble Theatre, Inc. (David Fishelson, Artistic Director; Seth A. Goldstein, Managing Director; Bess Eckstein, General Manager) on April 1, 2001. It was directed by Lawrence Sacharow; the set design was by Beowulf Boritt; the lighting design was by Michael Chybowski; the costume design was by Tracy Dorman; and the production stage manager was Alan Fox. The cast was as follows:

THE MAHARAL .... Robert Prosky
ISAAC / A MONK .... Michael Milligan
THE GOLEM .... Joseph McKenna
THADDEUS.. David Little
JACOB / THE MESSIAH .... Brandon Demery
THE REBBETSIN .... Lynn Cohen
DEVORALE .... Rosemary Garrison
REB BASSEVI / ELIJAH THE PROPHET .... Ben Hammer
TANKHUM .... Jeff Ware
SICK MAN.. Ian Pfister
BLIND MAN .... Steven Rosen
HUNCHBACK .... David Heuvelman
PEG LEG .... Stuart Rudin

CHARACTERS
(in order of appearance)

THE MAHARAL

ISAAC

A MONK

THE GOLEM

THADDEUS

JACOB

THE MESSIAH

THE REBBETSIN

DEVORALE

REB BASSEVI

ELIJAH THE PROPHET

TANKHUM

SICK MAN

BLIND MAN

HUNCHBACK

PEG LEG

JEWS OF PRAGUE

ANGRY MOB

PLACE

Prague, Czechoslovakia.

TIME

Late sixteenth century.

THE GOLEM

ACT ONE

Scene 1

A deserted place on the river outside of Prague, late sixteenth century. The hint of dawn breaking. All is silent. Rabbi Lev Bar-Bezalel, or the Maharal, stands over an outlined mound of clay, kneading the figure of a man. He finishes. Isaac, one of his students, stands near him, helping with the work. The Maharal then picks his staff up off the ground, uses it to straighten up.

MAHARAL.
(To Isaac.) It's done.
Now hurry to the synagogue
And bring Jacob with you.
ISAAC.
No one else, Rabbi?
MAHARAL.
No one —
And lock forever in your heart
What you've seen here tonight, Isaac.
ISAAC.
Forever, Rabbi.
MAHARAL.
Now go. *(Exit Isaac. The Maharal bends over the figure.)*
Yes, it's done —
The hour of wonder comes with morning.
This clay that I've shaped with my own hands,
I can discern the breath of life in it.

But how many ages has it slept here
While somewhere else its
Soul in longing wandered?
Or has the soul forgotten
The road's return to
Where the body sleeps? *(Looks up at the sky.)*
Yet who am I to say
That "My hands have shaped anything?"
Blind was I until *You* gave me sight — *(A rustle is heard and something completely dark suddenly appears beside the Maharal: the spirit of the unborn Golem.)*
Who goes there —
SPIRIT.
You don't know me?
MAHARAL.
I can't see your face.
SPIRIT.
You don't recognize my voice?
MAHARAL.
Speak, what's your name?
SPIRIT.
I'm still but a shadow.
Come to warn you: Create me not —
MAHARAL.
I order you to vanish —
SPIRIT.
— Create me not!
Where my foot will tread, a blight will grow
And what my hand will touch
Will crumble to dust and ash.
MAHARAL.
(Under his breath, fearfully.) Help me in this heaviest hour O Lord —
SPIRIT.
— The whole night through you molded me,
With coldness and with cruelty you shaped my form:
How good it was to be just clay
And lie there lifeless among the stones.

10

MAHARAL.
But I was sent by God to
Breathe the breath of life into you —
SPIRIT.
I don't want it —
MAHARAL.
But you've been created for more than just life:
In silence and secrecy you'll perform great deeds,
With no one knowing who the hero is
That protects them from the lies
And the burning of their temples:
You'll appear before the Jews
As but a carrier of water
And a cutter of wood:
But a savior you will be —
SPIRIT.
No: a Golem, a thing of clay.
MAHARAL.
A people's champion, a man of might.
SPIRIT.
A servant, to be ruled, and commanded.
MAHARAL.
A living man.
SPIRIT.
A living man?
Then why are my eyes still shut?
Why has no heart been given to me?
Where is the tongue and the blood
That must be poured to flow inside of me? *(Sees the sky.)*
Daylight — *(Suddenly afraid.)*
Oh darkness! Conceal me a moment longer! *(The Spirit dissolves
back into the darkness.)*
MAHARAL.
Something impure has invaded what
I strove so hard to render holy.
With words of fear I *myself*
Produced a flaw within the heart to be.
How many weeks, how many days and nights

Did I strive to purify my heart and mind, but now —
My own fear and doubt have tainted the spirit of this creature.
(Looks up at sky again.)
I am unworthy in Your eyes, O Lord:
Ambition is my curse, and pride as well.
I was too eager to see what
No man had seen before, but ...
Before *You*, what am *I*?
A worm, a lump of earth, a piece of dust — *(Enter Thaddeus the priest, wearing red robes and the cap of a high-ranking priest. He walks using a tall, thin cross-shaped staff. His entrance startles the Maharal.)*
THADDEUS.
(To the Maharal.) Well Rabbi:
What brings you here this middle of the night?
MAHARAL.
It isn't night, Thaddeus, but break of day.
THADDEUS.
(Ghost of a smile.) What brings you here at break of day, then?
MAHARAL.
I do at break of day what God commands.
THADDEUS.
And what did God command you to do?
Disobey the law and go outside
The ghetto walls before the sun is in the sky?
MAHARAL.
You speak, I think, of a man-made law
That lets ungodly deeds be done.
THADDEUS.
"Ungodly deeds"?
MAHARAL.
Yes: as recently as yesterday,
When a man — a member of your flock —
Reported the fact, so awful to discover:
Of the body of a Christian child —
The blood drained from its little corpse — filling twenty vials,
Found in the unlocked cellar of a wealthy Jew,
A pious man and father of two,
His property now split in perfect halves:

One parcel for the spy
And one for the state
While the innocent Jew was left to hang by his neck
Before his widow and children so that
Prague should bear witness
To his "crime of blood."
THADDEUS.
The Passover of the Jews
Is nigh, Rabbi, is it not? *(The Maharal goes pale with anger at the insolence of this remark.)*
MAHARAL.
(Shaking, but controlling himself.) That a Jew would mark a holy day
With anything but prayer and celebration —
THADDEUS.
(Slyly.) — And the making of unleavened bread
With just the right ingredient mix
Of blood and sinew, perhaps of bone —
MAHARAL.
— Is a libel that will never die!
And one that we must never again
Allow to pass for truth — !
THADDEUS.
(With the same curl of his lips.) All the same, Rabbi,
The Passover is nigh —
MAHARAL.
As too, perhaps, an era's end in which
My people go on, head bowed, to the slaughter.
THADDEUS.
An oratorical flourish, Rabbi,
And one well worthy of you!
MAHARAL.
You needn't stay, Thaddeus, go freely on your way.
THADDEUS.
That I can go my way is widely known.
It's my place as priest and
Guardian of the soul of Prague …
But what causes this strange look in *your* eyes:
A look of strength that gives me pause —

MAHARAL.
A "look" —
THADDEUS.
Yes: I've seen it in dungeons, and at the stake.
On the faces of so many Jews — a black strength …
And yet I've never seen two Jewish eyes
Look at me with such *hatred,* as yours do now. *(The Maharal
avoids Thaddeus' gaze; Thaddeus' lips twist into a smile.)*
You look away — ? *(His smile stops abruptly.)*
What's this — a corpse? *(Bends down, looks at the clay figure.)*
A figure made of clay…? *(Steps back and crosses himself.)*
O holy Jesus!
MAHARAL.
It's nothing —
THADDEUS.
(Hurrying away.) Protect me from the evil one,
From all who are unbaptized,
Cursed and damned, oh Christ! *(Exits.)*
MAHARAL. *(To himself, pacing nervously.)*
So it must be. The hand of God
Has wringed us round within a single ring.
Now let my heart be light and glad.
Let fear subside and strength remain behind
To shield us from the lies that would destroy us —
It must be! And it will! *(Turns at the sound of approaching footsteps.)*
ISAAC.
(Entering.) It's Isaac —
JACOB.
(Entering, following Isaac.) — and Jacob, your students —
MAHARAL.
(Going to meet them.) You come in time.
ISAAC.
The day breaks, Rabbi.
MAHARAL.
Did anyone see you?
JACOB.
No —

MAHARAL.
And were you in synagogue till now?
JACOB.
Yes, Rabbi.
ISAAC.
May we look — ?
MAHARAL.
Yes, but carefully — *(Both students bend over the figure.)*
JACOB.
There's not much to see. Just clay.
ISAAC.
But the clay moves — its eyes are opening —
JACOB.
It's moving its legs.
ISAAC.
Its face is contorting, it's — laughing?
MAHARAL.
Impossible — *(Isaac recoils.)*
What ails you, Isaac?
ISAAC.
A dream I once had, Rabbi —
The shape of the clay reminded me of it.
JACOB.
(Nervously.) In synagogue they spoke of evil times
In Prague, about a savage tyrant
Who slaughtered multitudes of Jews —
MAHARAL.
Yes, evil times will come
And with evil times come great ones too.
We must be ready to receive those days.
ISAAC.
(Holding forth a bundle.) Here is what you asked for.
MAHARAL.
Put it on the ground —
(Isaac lays the bundle on the ground.) Is everything contained in it?
ISAAC.
Everything —

JACOB.
Where will it stay, Rabbi?
MAHARAL.
"It"? *(Jacob nods down at the clay figure — the Maharal smiles faintly.)*
You mean "he."
JACOB.
"He"?
MAHARAL.
No more questions now. Contain your fears,
Or put them away in your hearts. *(He takes both by the elbows.)*
Now come to the river:
We'll wash our hands.

Scene 2

The Maharal's study. The Maharal enters, turns back toward the empty doorway … After a moment, the Golem appears: Three Hebrew letters are etched on his forehead: Aleph, Mem, Tet — "Emet," meaning "truth." He is taller than the doorway and does not know enough to bend.

MAHARAL.
Now bend your head. The door is low, and you
Are tall. Remember that, when one is tall
And wishes to come through a door that's low,
He must incline his head — like this. *(Shows how one bends his head. The Golem comes in stooping and remains so.)*
Now raise your head and stand up straight. *(The Golem straightens up. Remains silent. He is powerfully built — a giant. Large eyes. There is something heavy and dull about them and at the same time something childlike. Rather heavy lips with deep indentations at the corners. He has been dressed with ill-fitting bolts of dark cloth, hastily stitched. His eyes open ever wider as he stares at everything.)*

16

Now you've seen the sky
And the sun that rises in the east;
You've met Jews in the streets, and in the courtyards;
I've spoken to you; I speak to you again. *(The Golem is silent.)*
You have a mouth and tongue to speak, why are you silent? *(The Golem doesn't move.)*
Speak. I command you to speak.
Joseph is your name.
GOLEM.
(Uncertainly.) Joseph?
MAHARAL.
You're a man.
GOLEM.
A man.
MAHARAL.
You have a heart to live.
GOLEM.
To live.
MAHARAL.
You recall your name — ? *(The Golem is silent.)*
You've forgotten. "Joseph." Remember it.
GOLEM.
Joseph.
MAHARAL.
And do you know what I am called?
GOLEM.
Rabbi. *(The Golem suddenly begins to stride around the room, knocking over benches. He presses against the wall, pushes it. The windows rattle.)*
MAHARAL.
Stop — you'll wake up everyone.
GOLEM.
I want to leave this place. *(Strikes the wall.)*
MAHARAL.
One cannot penetrate a wall.
I tell you — stop.
GOLEM.
I want to leave this place.

17

MAHARAL.
I told you on the way here
That you must carry out what I command.
GOLEM. *(Stands still, looking helpless.)* I'll obey, Rabbi.
MAHARAL.
You must always hear my words. Do you recall your name?
GOLEM.
Yes ... "Joseph."
MAHARAL.
Go and sit on that bench. *(When the Golem doesn't move, the Maharal takes him by the hand, guides him toward the bench.)*
You're tired. You come from far away:
But don't fear, you're a welcome guest.
GOLEM.
A welcome guest.
MAHARAL.
I found you on the outskirts of the town.
You were asleep.
GOLEM.
(Ignoring him, staring off.) Fire from somewhere, it's on the windows,
It's getting red. And the walls —
They start to burn. Your face burns too — *(Jumps up.)*
MAHARAL.
Where are you going?
GOLEM.
To the fire. I'm afraid to stay.
MAHARAL.
(Grabbing his arm.) You can't go.
GOLEM.
But I want to go.
MAHARAL.
Have you forgotten who I am?
GOLEM.
I don't know.
MAHARAL.
You're my servant.
You've come into my house.
You're under my command.

GOLEM.

What must I do?

MAHARAL.

Nothing yet. Not till you're ready.

And I will tell you when that is.

GOLEM.

(Looking round.) The fire returns. The walls conspire with the door to

Hurl themselves upon me. Let me go —

MAHARAL.

I can't —

GOLEM.

(Getting agitated again.) I want to twist

My head off my shoulders, twist my arms and legs,

Put out the fire around me.

Take away the walls — ! *(He hurls himself wildly against the wall, smashes it with his fists. The walls shake.)*

MAHARAL.

(Angrily.) Be calm, I say! Be calm! *(He puts his hands on the Golem's head, which calms him.)*

My first blessing,

Let it fall upon your heart and disheveled thoughts,

Is that you're my guest. A welcome guest.

Let that alone suffice for you to feel hope. *(Footsteps approach.)*

You've awakened my wife and daughter:

You're a guest and come from foreign parts,

Let that be your reply. *(The Maharal stands, as the Rebbetsin, his wife (in her forties) and Devorale, his daughter (around eighteen) enter looking frightened, startled from their sleep.)*

REBBETSIN.

What's wrong? What was it shook the house?

DEVORALE.

Such screaming, Father —

REBBETSIN.

(Noticing the Golem.) Who is this, Arye Levi? Who sits here?

DEVORALE.

How strange he looks —

MAHARAL.

A stranger, and now our guest.

I saw him lying on the bare ground,
Exhausted from his travels.
DEVORALE.
The word written on his forehead: the word "truth"?
Why is it written there, Father?
REBBETSIN.
Such hands, such shoulders this man has.
This is not a Jew ...
He frightens me —
MAHARAL.
No need to be afraid,
The dust of the road is still upon him, that's all —
DEVORALE.
See how he stares at me, Mother,
What does he want?
REBBETSIN.
Don't stare back, child,
He's a poor man and should be pitied, and yet —
He makes me uneasy.
Stranger, what's your name?
GOLEM.
Joseph. (*He rises and looks intently at Devorale.*)
Rabbi, who is she?
Why is she fearful, why does she move away?
DEVORALE.
Hide me, Mother, he frightens me.
REBBETSIN.
The child is frightened — is he mad or what?
MAHARAL.
Why do you stare so, Joseph?
GOLEM.
Who is she, Rabbi? Why does she want to get away?
MAHARAL.
(*Under his breath.*) She's my daughter, do you hear?
Don't speak to her again —
GOLEM.
Her long hair hangs down over her shoulders.

DEVORALE.

What's he saying, Mother — ?

REBBETSIN.

It's disgraceful for him to speak so —

MAHARAL.

He doesn't know what comes out of his mouth.

His mind isn't clear.

GOLEM.

(Suddenly.) Food.

MAHARAL.

Food? Yes, bring him some.

REBBETSIN.

Before morning prayers?

MAHARAL.

It doesn't matter —

REBBETSIN.

Then I'll bring a bite for him myself — *(To Devorale, as she takes her by the arm:)*

— You must go back to sleep. *(Exit the Rebbetsin and Devorale.)*

GOLEM.

Where did she go?

MAHARAL.

To bring you food.

GOLEM.

And then she'll stay? She won't leave?

MAHARAL.

I've told you once: She's my daughter.

Don't speak or think of her.

GOLEM.

(Sadly.) I felt good each time she looked at me.

MAHARAL.

Be still!

GOLEM.

Can't I take her by the hand?

MAHARAL.

(Furiously.) No! Nor look at her again! Recall,

A different life is yours to live,

A different air to breathe,

Till then, be mute. Be locked within your muteness.
GOLEM.
Speak to no one?
MAHARAL.
Just answer when you're spoken to. No more.
And keep yourself aloof from people. When you
Go into the synagogue or elsewhere,
Take your place unnoticed, in some corner.
If one approaches you to ask a question,
Answer without anger. To be set apart
Is neither punishment nor grief —
It's but the road that you must take
To wonder and to glory for our people.
GOLEM.
(Sits down, turns head away.) It's getting dark for me.
I can't see at all.
I'm falling, Rabbi, I'm sure that I'm falling ...
MAHARAL.
You're not falling, you're just hungry. *(The Rebbetsin comes in followed by Devorale. The Rebbetsin brings bread, a pitcher of water and a bowl, and sets all this down in front of the Golem. He doesn't move.)*
REBBETSIN.
Won't our guest wash? *(The Golem remains motionless.)*
What ails him, Arye Levi?
DEVORALE.
Is he asleep?
REBBETSIN.
Honored guest, wash for eating. *(Pause — she pours water into the bowl.)*
Here is water.
Why is he silent? *(The Golem raises his eyes but says nothing.)*
You want to eat — then wash.
MAHARAL.
Wash, Joseph. *(The Golem drops his hands into the bowl, promptly knocking it over: It clangs to the floor. The Rebbetsin holds out a towel for him. He stares at the towel, doesn't take it, turns to the food and begins eating hungrily.)*

REBBETSIN.
(Dismayed.) No blessing for the bread — ?
MAHARAL.
The synagogue must have someone
To carry water, cut the wood.
I have long needed a servant,
A man of strength like him.
REBBETSIN.
He gave the child a fright, God knows —
MAHARAL.
Lucky was the hour
That God put him in our path.
REBBETSIN.
If you know best, husband,
Then I will worry less … *(To the Golem.)*
Should I bring you something more to eat? *(The Golem stares at her, not answering, then cranes his neck so he can see Devorale, hiding behind her mother.)*
DEVORALE.
Still his eyes are glued to me.
MAHARAL.
Both of you: Go now. *(Devorale and the Rebbetsin exit. To the Golem:)*
Well, have you had your fill?
GOLEM.
My eyes feel heavy, Rabbi.
MAHARAL.
Good. You'll sleep
And when you wake,
The world will seem quite different. *(The Golem nods, dozing. He falls asleep sitting up.)*
So much anguish in this face …
(The Maharal stares at the Golem, watching him sleep.)
Is this the hero I dreamt into existence?
Such hands, such shoulders,
So much body — ? *(He listens to the Golem's deep, heavy breathing.)*
So much still sorrow…?

Scene 3

The Maharal's study. Evening. The Maharal, having dozed with his forehead resting on his hands, slumped at a table, is agitated and mumbling in his sleep, while Devorale is shaking him, trying to wake him.

DEVORALE.
Father, wake up —
MAHARAL.
(Awakening.) What —
DEVORALE.
You were crying out in your sleep —
MAHARAL.
A dream, child, that's all —
DEVORALE.
"Fire and blood!" you shouted,
And something about "Tower Five — "
MAHARAL.
A nightmare, it's nothing,
Just an old man with troubled sleep.
Go see to your mother — *(Devorale kisses his forehead, then exits. The Maharal lays his head back down on the table, his face resting on his hands again. The Golem enters softly and stands near the door. He holds an axe in his hand. He scrutinizes the Maharal. The more he looks, the more Golem-like the expression on his face becomes. He walks softly over to the table, sits down on the bench directly opposite, and imitates the way the Maharal rests his head on the table. A while passes like this ... The Maharal suddenly looks up with a start, sees the Golem.)*
MAHARAL.
Good heavens, why are you here?
GOLEM.
I saw you sleeping, Rabbi. Sitting.

MAHARAL.
You needn't imitate all that I do.
Why did you come here?
GOLEM.
You called me.
MAHARAL.
When did I call you?
GOLEM.
Quite a while now ...
I heard you calling me: "Joseph — "
MAHARAL.
(Sternly.) I didn't call you.
Now go back to work:
Have you split all the rails?
GOLEM.
They don't let me work.
MAHARAL.
Who doesn't?
GOLEM.
The boys. The grown-ups too.
They ask me what my name is.
MAHARAL.
Don't answer them.
GOLEM.
I don't answer.
You told me to keep quiet.
MAHARAL.
They won't harm you.
GOLEM.
I hate them.
MAHARAL.
(After pause.) You must live peaceably with everyone.
GOLEM.
(Going over to the window.) You see: They're staring at me
Through the window now —
MAHARAL.
I myself will go out and tell them to stop.

25

GOLEM.
They don't fear you either.
I say: The Rabbi will come out and scold you,
And when I say that, they laugh even more —
I think ... that if they feel they
Have to laugh then I should
Take the axe to one of their necks
If that will stop the laughter.
MAHARAL.
(Rising angrily to his feet.) What are you saying!?
Not for one second will you consider
The spilling of Jewish blood!!
For this you were given life!?
GOLEM.
(In anguish.) Then take them away from me!
Why do they talk and stare?
Why do you say I can't raise my axe,
When, by itself, my axe rises in my hands?
MAHARAL.
By itself?
I gave your arms their strength,
"Let the axe be a feather in your hand" —
Such was my blessing to you! *(Struggling to calm himself, he sits.)*
But now I see it must be otherwise ...
So I command you:
Let every axe-lift be heavy toil —
To keep the lightness of your arm from temptation. *(Wiping sweat from his brow, he's exhausted by this outburst.)*
Go back to work and pay no heed to anyone —
GOLEM.
(After pause.) If you were always with me,
I wouldn't be afraid ...
Don't send me away from you.
MAHARAL.
I'm not sending you away. You see me
So many times each day.
I can't always be with you.
Know that you came here to be alone.

Go do the work you do, and
When you're finished — go to sleep in Tower Five —
GOLEM.
Tower Five?
MAHARAL.
The Fifth Tower:
The palace ruins inside the ghetto
Where Jewish beggars now find a place to lie
And rest between their wretched rounds —
GOLEM.
And that's where I must go — ?
MAHARAL.
Isaac will conduct you there
And make a sleeping place for you.
You surely don't want me there to sleep beside you —
GOLEM.
(After pause.) Why: Is there not room enough for two?
MAHARAL.
You must be with yourself
And not with me.
I took you for a servant not that I
Might follow you and watch you as you eat and sleep.
I'll call you when I need you. Now go. *(Exit Golem, axe in hand.)*
Helpless himself — he must bring help to us.
Yet he who is to save us is the first to cry for help ...
I sent him out in anger; yet he did no wrong. *(He looks out the window.)*
You stamped the sorrow of a feeble mind upon him,
So that we might not know the greatness
That is his. No doubt it should be so. *(Reb Bassevi enters, a middle-aged Jew, richly dressed.)*
REB BASSEVI.
Good evening, Rabbi.
MAHARAL.
Ah Reb Bassevi — a good year to you —
REB BASSEVI.
And you, Rabbi.
I crossed the courtyard of the synagogue,

And saw the knots of men in earnest talk.
They wonder and they worry,
Rumors rush from mouth to mouth
Of loss of fortune due to
Infant bodies, drained of life
That find themselves inside our homes.
MAHARAL.
The homes in which our wives
Themselves have given birth —
REB BASSEVI.
The very same: If you could've seen
The turmoil in the courtyard —
That woodcutter came along
And scared them all to death.
MAHARAL.
You, too, Reb Bassevi? A man
At work, chopping wood. What cause is there for fear?
We've long sought an able woodman —
REB BASSEVI.
But this man it seems
Has not found favor.
You should have seen them all
Come pouring, young and old,
From every house to gape at him —
Who is he, Rabbi? Do you know?
MAHARAL.
He comes from foreign parts, but that's no matter.
Tell everyone:
There's no cause for fear.
REB BASSEVI.
I'll tell them —
MAHARAL.
But still you're uneasy, Reb Bassevi.
REB BASSEVI.
Forgive me, Rabbi.
Last night, I couldn't close my eyes till dawn.
I can't be certain
If we ourselves magnify the danger

Or whether the opposite is true.
What if the danger far exceeds our fears?
Who knows what traps are daily set for the Jews?
Who knows what hands will bring catastrophe?
What do they want of us, Rabbi? Tell me,
I mean quite simply, I wish to understand:
What do they want of us?
MAHARAL.
(In a voice overwhelmed with emotion.)
They want so much of us, so very much.
But we can give them nothing.
Or maybe we can. Indeed, we can:
But we do not want to. *We do not want to.*
With but one fingertip
We touched the world and everything it holds.
Standing at the side, we merely breathed upon it,
And all the world and everything it holds
Will forever bear the imprint of our breath.
So why should we ask questions what they want of *us*?
If we desire, we turn our face in greeting to the world.
If not, we turn our back to it.
The world is but a passageway, an anteroom for us.
Perhaps that passage is too long,
Too littered and cluttered with axes and spears.
But who will clear away those axes
If, with the axes, he must clean away
Our touch as well?
Beyond that, we can liberate the world:
We can, but we refuse.
REB BASSEVI.
Refuse?
MAHARAL.
Yes, for this is precisely what *they* would want.
To free the world as they desire
Means: to free the world of us.
REB BASSEVI.
I hear, and every word lashes
The anguish of my heart.

MAHARAL.
Anguish? We have grown into it, grown part of it,
Wrapped it round us, set the torch to it
And scattered its light throughout the world.
Your face glows with this anguish, Reb Bassevi —
But an hour of impatience may come,
An hour of stubbornness where
Instead of brushing one fingertip against the world
We might instead raise our hand up whole,
With all its fingers clenched downward into a fist!
What do you think would happen then, Reb Bassevi,
What would happen then!?
REB BASSEVI.
Catastrophe! Catastrophe for us —
MAHARAL.
Catastrophe?
Catastrophe is when we die like cattle instead of men —
REB BASSEVI.
It's true, we need not die like cattle:
But nor should we resort to living like beasts —
Won't those who lift the sword fare worse?
In doing so won't they lose their share of the world to come — ?
MAHARAL.
Whether in this world or the next, Reb Bassevi:
There may be no tomorrow for Jews
Who meekly lay their necks upon the block … *(Pacing agitatedly.)*
What if it were not I,
Or you or someone else
But he, that very woodman in the yard,
Who raised his hands with all his fingers
Stretched outward in defiance —! *(Stops abruptly, hearing something.)*
REB BASSEVI.
Rabbi — the blood is draining from your face —
MAHARAL.
(Listening.) A noise, do you hear it?
REB BASSEVI.
I hear no noise.

MAHARAL.
Did I imagine it...? *(Looks out the window.)*
The Jews in synagogue are finishing their prayers
And soon will all go home to bed.
But, perhaps, like you
They won't close their eyes tonight.
REB BASSEVI.
I was hoping to hear words of comfort —
MAHARAL.
Instead bear *these* words in mind:
No longer lie awake the whole night through.
A Jew must never keep himself from sleep.
One must never grow too tired to apprehend all wonders.
Do you understand? All wonders —
REB BASSEVI.
(Uncertainly.) I'm not sure, Rabbi,
But you seem unafraid
And I will share that spirit with the rest of them — *(A commotion is heard outside the door. The Maharal opens the door and looks out.)*
MAHARAL.
What's going on out there? Tankhum? *(Tankhum stumbles in, disheveled and tattered; a madman, but one who is mad from grief. One of his lapels is ripped in sign of mourning.)*
TANKHUM.
Such impudence! Tankhum wants to see the Rabbi,
And they won't let him!
MAHARAL.
You're here now, Tankhum, sit down, sit down —
TANKHUM.
No time to sit, Rabbi.
I have to hurry,
My chariot is waiting —
REB BASSEVI.
Will there be no limit to your mourning?
TANKHUM.
A limit? No, there's no limit.
Had it not been for our great festival of Passover
My son Daniel would still be alive;

31

Should we therefore wash our hands of Passover?
REB BASSEVI.
We've heard this all before, Tankhum —
TANKHUM.
Impossible!
How can the deaf hear?
How can the blind see?
Five is the number of towers —
Five.
One for the east and one for the west,
One for the north and one for the south.
The fifth one — is for me.
MAHARAL.
(Wrinkling his brow.) Why do you speak of the Fifth Tower?
TANKHUM.
Who suffers the grief of the towers?
I do!
I'm the lord of the ruins!
MAHARAL.
That's enough, rest yourself —
TANKHUM.
All have gone
Into the synagogue for evening prayers
Leaving me alone with him — that cut-throat.
But I have no fear of cut-throats.
Even those with truth written on their foreheads.
And this is what I came to tell you:
That I have no fear of axes.
REB BASSEVI.
You hear this, Rabbi?
MAHARAL.
Why do you speak these words, Tankhum?
TANKHUM.
Why?
You ask that, Rabbi?
Darkness is coming upon us, darkness
From all sides,
Let axes lift,

Voices shout —
Hands grow tired,
Axes rust,
Throats get silent,
And if not silent — they get cut. *(Grabbing the Maharal's arm.)*
Who is master here?
You, Rabbi? Or Thaddeus the Priest?
Did you know that
Thaddeus comes to Tower Five?
Did you know that, Rabbi?
MAHARAL.
Yes, he wants to drive the paupers out —
TANKHUM.
He wants to drive
The *Jewish* paupers out!
Out of a palace no one uses!
But who is master there? He or you?
Or is it the woodcutter, perhaps — ? *(Letting go of the Maharal's arm.)*
In my chariot
Lies my son,
His left eye, run through by a spear,
His right one — closed.
His right arm lopped off at the shoulder,
His left one — at the elbow.
Each first night of Passover I tell my son:
Arise and be alive.
And he rises up,
And he waits,
Until we hear footsteps:
And then ...
Again they stab his left eye through,
Hack his right arm at the elbow,
Hack his left one at the shoulder.
And I lay him back into the chariot again
And say: next year ... in Jerusalem ...
Because my heart is filled with pity for the world ... *(Tankhum weeps uncontrollably ... then suddenly runs from the room — exits. The Maharal and Reb Bassevi stare after him in amazement. A long*

silence. The Maharal gets up, starts to pace the room.)
MAHARAL.
(Muttering angrily.) They drive us mad with violence,
While the threat of more to come infects our minds — *(Stops pacing, points after the departed Tankhum:)*
That one there was once quite sane:
A father and a man of prayer — ! *(The Maharal raises his fist to his mouth as if to bottle up the anger.)*
REB BASSEVI.
(Standing up to leave.) The evening prayers will soon begin.
For now, Rabbi —
MAHARAL.
I will follow soon. *(Exit Reb Bassevi. The Maharal continues pacing, then stops at the window. From the courtyard, uneasy voices of men and women are heard crying: "Where is the Rabbi? Rabbi, please come out." Women's voices: "Heaven help us! Such grief upon us!" The Maharal starts toward the door. The Rebbetsin enters, holding the weeping Devorale in her arms. Both are terrified.)*
MAHARAL.
(Taking Devorale in his arms.) What happened?
REBBETSIN.
The new man, that woodman, heaven help us —
MAHARAL.
What has he done?
REBBETSIN.
She went outside for water,
But he wouldn't let her near the well —
DEVORALE.
(Weeping.) He said that he must carry water —
MAHARAL.
And then — ?
REBBETSIN.
It's disgraceful just to speak of it.
In sight of all he grabbed her,
Threw his arms around her, and
Hugged her to his breast.
MAHARAL.
And what is he doing now?

REBBETSIN.

What should he do? A golem, not a man!

He stands immobile, turned to stone.

DEVORALE.

Drive him away Father, make him go — ! *(She breaks down weeping.)*

MAHARAL.

(To the Rebbetsin.) Take her now, and make her rest.

The potions, you know where they keep —

While I attend to making this home safe

For her and you and I. *(The Rebbetsin shakes her head, leads her daughter out. The moment they leave, the Maharal turns and yells furiously out the window:)*

Come up here now! Joseph! *(He paces, angry and impatient. Then the Golem enters, carrying his axe. He stands in the middle of the room, curiously rigid, his hands hanging at his sides. The Maharal studies him for a while, takes the axe from his hand, sets it down on a bench.)*

Lift your head and raise your eyes. *(The Golem doesn't move. The Maharal picks up his staff and walks around him.)*

I prayed to God for wonders —

But you stand there stiff as wood;

Your eyes are dull, your mouth distorted.

Your shoulders, like lifeless walls of clay

While primordial, dust-encrusted worms

Still crawl across your arms

And from your breath erupts the stench of rotting earth!

Your life is only one day old

And yet how soon the man in you has hurried to reveal himself

In hatred, passion, and misfortune.

Did I bring you here that you might be like other men!?

Where on your face is the gleaming light and radiant glow

Of our common trust and faith?

Why are you dumb? Reply!

Reply, before I raise my staff against you! *(As he raises his staff to strike, the Golem suddenly comes to — gulping/inhaling some too-long held breath while stretching out his hand in innocent joy to the Maharal.)*

GOLEM.

Where am I, Rabbi, where did they all go?

Everyone was shouting so

I couldn't understand why it suddenly grew so still …
Was I asleep?
MAHARAL.
Asleep?
GOLEM.
It was *my* throat that someone's hands were choking.
I thought at first that they were yours …
Oh stay with me and do not leave — *(He stretches full length upon the floor at the Maharal's feet.)*
Stay with me, or else — drive me away.
MAHARAL.
Get up. I see your grief —
I forgive you.
GOLEM.
Just do not leave me.
MAHARAL.
Stand up.
GOLEM.
Let me lie here at your feet.
MAHARAL.
In the name of God, stand up. *(Sadly, stiffly, the Golem stands up, his eyes closed.)*
Now open your eyes. *(The Golem does so.)*
Behold the light, and do not fear:
It's time for you to sleep again.
Go forth unto the Fifth Tower:
There you'll stay, and there you'll sleep. *(The Golem walks slowly out of the room. As he exits, the Maharal sinks back down on a chair by the table. He leans forward and lets his forehead rest on his hands, resuming the position of anguished sleep in which we found him at the scene's beginning. But he can't sleep — so he sits back up and starts rubbing his eyes in frustration.)*

Scene 4

In the Fifth Tower. A large room, a shambles. On both sides,
entrances to other rooms. One wall has been broken through.
The others are blackened, covered with cobwebs, soaked by
the rains. No doors, shaky thresholds, broken windows. In
various places, perhaps, signs of former murals. They are all
smeared and covered with stains and careless scratches. In one
corner there still hang the chains of sacred lamps.

Paupers and beggars live in the room. On the floor, where
they sleep, old rags, bundles, torn pillows lie about.

The night has just begun. A cold wind howls through the
windows. It's very dark in the room.

A sick pauper, feverish, lies in a corner in a tangle of rags.
The rest have not yet arrived.

SICK MAN.
How cold it is. No food today — *(Sits up.)*
Is anyone there? *(Lies down again.)*
Why do they take so long to come?
I have no strength to stand and light the lamp
Or stuff the gaping windows.
Help me sleep, God of Abraham, Isaac, and Jacob — *(Covers him-*
self with the rags lying near him, huddles under them and shivers.
Silence. The Golem enters. Stops in the middle of the room. Does not
know which way to turn. Says nothing. The Sick Man raises his head.)
Has someone come, thank God? *(The Golem says nothing.)*
Have you no tongue to answer a sick man? *(With growing fear.)*
Who are you?
Why have you come to Tower Five? *(Sits up and looks at the Golem.*
His fright increases.)

Why don't you speak? *(The Golem turns away from the Sick Man, walks off to a far corner.)*
A place to sleep, is that what you want here?
GOLEM.
Don't speak to me.
SICK MAN.
Where do you come from?
GOLEM.
Don't speak to me. *(The Sick Man sinks back to the floor and stares fearfully at the Golem. The Golem can scarcely be seen in the darkness. The Hunchback and the Blind Man enter. The Sick Man falls asleep.)*
BLIND MAN.
But are you sure?
HUNCHBACK.
How could one mistake a priest?
BLIND MAN.
Then it's true.
You say he walked behind us?
HUNCHBACK.
No more than twenty paces,
With staff in hand,
Then he turned and made
His way back to Prague.
BLIND MAN.
It was Thaddeus?
HUNCHBACK.
The same.
BLIND MAN.
Then God has punished me. For I can't see the ones who follow us. *(Suddenly.)*
Are we alone?
HUNCHBACK.
(Looking.) The sick one's here. Asleep.
BLIND MAN.
Besides the sick one?
HUNCHBACK.
That's all.

BLIND MAN.
(Sensing the Golem's presence.) Are you sure? Look around —
HUNCHBACK.
What do you mean? *(The Blind Man taps around with his staff. It touches the Sick Man, who awakens.)*
SICK MAN.
A little water, I beg you —
HUNCHBACK.
There's no water.
SICK MAN.
Careful: There's a stranger here —
HUNCHBACK.
A stranger? Here in Tower Five?
BLIND MAN.
(Nervously.) I told you —
HUNCHBACK.
(Suddenly seeing the Golem in silhouette, sitting in the corner.) It's him, that woodcutter,
The one who grabbed the Rabbi's daughter —
SICK MAN.
His name is "Joseph" —
BLIND MAN.
Shh: Speak softly —
How did he get here? *(The Golem gets to his feet with a groan.)*
What's that, is it him — ?
GOLEM.
You say my name —
SICK MAN.
Your name? No. I only said —
GOLEM.
Don't say it again. *(Sits back down in shadow.)*
HUNCHBACK.
(In a harsh whisper to the Blind Man.) You can thank God
You're blind and can't see him.
BLIND MAN.
But the Rabbi himself befriended him —
SICK MAN.
(Muttering.) God of Abraham, Isaac, and Jacob — *(The three beg-*

gars sit as far away from the Golem as they can get. The Blind Man takes a little bag out of his breast pocket, unties it.)
HUNCHBACK.
(Shaking some coins out of his own bag; to the Blind Man.)
You made a lot, didn't you? I didn't get a penny —
BLIND MAN.
(Touching at his own coins.) How would I know whether it's a lot?
(Suddenly a noise at the entry: In hobbles the Peg Leg.)
PEG LEG.
Greetings, Jews —
BLIND MAN.
We have a guest, a guest —
PEG LEG.
What guest?
HUNCHBACK.
The woodman from the prayer-house yard.
PEG LEG.
Is it true? The whole of Prague is buzzing about him.
SICK MAN.
There he sits. Hiding in the dark.
Staring at us.
PEG LEG.
(Seeing the Golem.) What a size!
BLIND MAN.
Shh: He might hear you. It's not safe.
PEG LEG.
Why? Will he strike you with his axe?
HUNCHBACK.
He doesn't have to:
One look from his eyes is
Enough to kill you.
PEG LEG.
What's his name?
SICK MAN.
(Whispering.) They say it's "Joseph." *(The Golem stands up again.)*
GOLEM.
You say my name again.
Say it no more. *(The Golem exits the room.)*

SICK MAN.
That's the second time today!
And twice to me. He must be mad!
I thought I whispered —
BLIND MAN.
Is there a law against saying a man's name?
HUNCHBACK.
The Rabbi sent him here himself.
PEG LEG.
The Rabbi himself? *(They all look at each other ... then settle back down to untying their bags, etc.)*
HUNCHBACK.
(To Peg Leg.) You met nobody on the way?
The priest was behind us.
PEG LEG.
Who? Thaddeus?
HUNCHBACK.
He wants to drive us out of here.
BLIND MAN.
Expel us? From this place?
It's in the ghetto, isn't it?
You can be driven from a house,
But who can drive you from a ruin?
It's why Tower Five
Is so packed with Jews!
SICK MAN.
Supposing, God forbid, they come
To drive us from this place as well? *(The Golem, without warning, enters again, stands hulking just inside the doorway. All go motionless with fear. Suddenly Tankhum comes in the same doorway. His eyes scan everyone. He turns and sees the Golem, then walks up close to him and bursts out laughing.)*
SICK MAN.
(To Tankhum.) What are you laughing at, you lunatic?
TANKHUM.
(To the Golem.) Do you know them? *(Points to all of them.)*
Do you know who they are?
You see that hunchback?

You see that wooden leg —
Go ahead: Split it with your axe!
You know how wood is split! *(The Golem says nothing, stares ...
Then slowly, the Golem turns and starts to exit. Tankhum, yelling at
the Golem's exiting back:)*
Remember, I'm the master here!
These broken windows are all mine.
But in seven days
He will rise.
From the flaming chariot he'll come;
For Tower Five belongs to him,
To him — my heir!
Don't you hear these ruins shouting,
"When will he be here?"
Tie up your bags,
Make clean this house
For he is coming — ! *(Enter suddenly two wandering paupers,
strangers, the Old Beggar and the Young Beggar — Elijah the Prophet
and the Messiah — though naturally, the audience has no inkling yet
of their identities. They come with bags on their backs and staffs in
hand, dusty from their long journey and very tired. Tankhum appears
completely stunned by their sudden appearance.)*
OLD BEGGAR.
*Shalom aleichem, Jews, aleichem shalom. (The Old Beggar greets
them all with a handshake and* "shalom aleichem." *All but Tankhum
respond in kind.)*
Can we spend the night here?
PEG LEG.
Uncle, you can even sleep here many nights —
These ruins can accommodate us all.
OLD BEGGAR.
We need to spend just one night here, no more,
And with the day we must be on our way again.
We're fatigued. He — even more.
He's still young and unaccustomed to the road. *(They drop their
bags and prepare to seat themselves.)*
HUNCHBACK.
(Helping the Young Beggar sit.) He looks ill.

OLD BEGGAR.
From the long road his feet have broken out in sores —
He needs to rest —
SICK MAN.
You're in a hurry?
OLD BEGGAR.
No, not in a hurry any more.
We drove ourselves to come here. These last days
Both day and night we walked.
From now on we no longer have to hurry.
BLIND MAN.
But what drove you here?
PEG LEG.
Yes: Is there something
Here in Prague that you require?
OLD BEGGAR.
Not require, no, but need:
Yes, we need to be where we are needed.
HUNCHBACK.
(Peering at the Young Beggar's face.) He doesn't look like any beggar.
His face is too refined.
YOUNG BEGGAR.
(Quietly.) How tired I am … And weary —
BLIND MAN.
(Stunned.) Who is that just spoke?
I know that voice!
YOUNG BEGGAR.
My eyelids … heavy …
BLIND MAN.
Why would *he* be *here?*
It can't be him —
OLD BEGGAR.
(To the Young Beggar.) Sleep — *(Places a bag under the Young Beggar's head.)*
Sleep well.
TANKHUM.
(Jumps up.) Guests come to spend the night here,
And no one asks permission!

43

I'm still the master here!
SICK MAN.
Quiet! Can't you see this man is sleeping?
TANKHUM.
Asleep?
He has to wake up! And anyway, this isn't a man —
Not what you and I would call a man! *(To the Old Beggar.)*
Tell me if I'm wrong —
Tell me you're not Elijah
And this the Messiah you have brung — !
HUNCHBACK.
(Giving Tankhum a shove.) Madman! Shut your mouth!
OLD MAN.
Don't strike him, please —
HUNCHBACK.
But I tell you, it's impossible to stand him!
With his words and curses and maddened talk —
TANKHUM. *(Still lying on the floor, shouting.)*
But why should he sleep?
He's come to save us all!
Ask the one who wields the axe — *(Seeing a figure in the doorway.)*
No: The Rabbi ye shall ask! *(The Maharal is there — suddenly — standing half-silhouetted in the doorway.)*
ALL.
(Surprised.) Rabbi! The Rabbi!
MAHARAL.
(To the Old Beggar after a long silence.) Why are you here?
Why have you both come here?
Who sent you? Who ordered you to come?
OLD BEGGAR.
Only to spend the night.
One night to rest on our long road —
MAHARAL.
You came yourselves? At no one's bidding!
Pick up your bags at once
And go. I order it to be so.
OLD BEGGAR.
We're exhausted from our journey.

Our haste was great —
MAHARAL.
(Struggling to be firm, lest he be swayed.) You hurried here?
Then hurry back again. I order it.
OLD BEGGAR.
(Looking at the Young Beggar.) He sleeps so soundly. Don't wake him.
MAHARAL.
Are there no ruins elsewhere in the world? *(Pounds with his staff.)*
To come unbidden! Unbidden! *(The Golem enters, stands at the Maharal's side. When the Old Beggar sees the Golem, he changes completely. He grows pale, begins to tremble, and quickly starts to wake the Young Beggar.)*
OLD BEGGAR.
Wake up! Wake up! Be quick!
We have to leave — *(Starts to gather his things together.)*
YOUNG BEGGAR.
A little while longer — *(Suddenly, the Young Beggar sees the Golem, and his look of exhaustion quickly becomes one of compassion. He rises achingly to his feet, reaches out his hand. The Golem reaches out his hand also. The Young Beggar's fingertips touch the fingertips of the Golem. The two hold this position as all in the room freeze and stare. Then the Young Beggar slowly drops his hand. Leaning on the Old Beggar, and limping as he goes, he exits with the Old Beggar, who carries both their bundles. The Maharal looks away, unable to bear the sight of their departure. The Golem starts after them.)*
MAHARAL.
(Restraining him.) Where to?
GOLEM.
With them. I want to be with them.
MAHARAL.
Stay here, I order you. *Their* time
Has not yet come. This is *your* time — *(The Golem, with a sad look, finally stops straining against the Maharal's grip, stares at the floor. The Maharal addresses the room:)*
There is a God in heaven, Jews.
Sleep well.
BLIND MAN.
A God in heaven.

PEG LEG.

Thank you, Rabbi. *(The beggars start to make their "beds." Tankhum doesn't move from his place on the floor. The Maharal stares at Tankhum, who stares back defiantly. The Maharal then takes the Golem aside, so that none of the beggars can hear him.)*

MAHARAL.

(To the Golem.) Will you know what you have to do?

GOLEM.

I'll know, Rabbi.

MAHARAL.

But not to the death.

GOLEM.

No Rabbi, not to the death.

MAHARAL.

(Firmly gripping the Golem's head.) Your power to be invisible —
Now is the time for that! *(The Maharal stares into the Golem's eyes ... then releases him and exits. The beggars finally settle in for sleep, as Tankhum gets up and also exits, following the Maharal. A few moments pass, underscored by an eerie, ethereal music reminiscent of chanting. It grows darker. ... A noise of several approaching footsteps. Thaddeus enters with rapid steps, accompanied by a Monk. The beggars rise in startled fear. The Golem is no longer seen. ...)*

THADDEUS.

You see these beggars? Pretenders every one.
Believe me, they're wealthier than both of us.
You see that hump? That hump is false —
A pack of rags, no more.

MONK.

Then he's quite an artist.

THADDEUS.

And this one — he's not blind at all.
He keeps his eyes shut
That he might find his way.

MONK.

(Pointing to Peg Leg.) Well there's one, Father, you can't suspect.
That leg is wood, all right.

THADDEUS.

Don't you believe it.

His kind can amputate a leg
And keep it hidden in a bag
And when they need it, take it out again.
They live like kings up here as though they owned the place.
The walls are filthy, full of nails;
The air so foul it takes your breath away.
To think that here once lived in glory
Our gentlemen and nobles!
That these louse-ridden floors
Once felt the step of royal feet.
Now all is ruin. *He* has been cast out,
The tears that dripped in sorrow from His crown of thorns,
Which they, grim unbelievers, stuck into His brow. *(To the beggars.)*
Why do you gape and stand around?
You live among us, angry and embittered,
And wear your anger as he wears his hump.
Haven't we tortured you enough,
Oppressed you, burnt you, led you out to slaughter?
We've grown weary of our hatred,
Yet still you parade your zealotry before us
And clench your teeth in obstinate tenacity —
And all the more, you smash our dreams of peace,
And all the more, you stoke in us the fires of hate.
No peace can ever be between us —
You haunt us like an evil dream.
We cannot share one Earth with you,
Warmed by the same sun, breathing the same air.
The air your lungs inhale becomes noxious to our hearts;
And our hearts yearn for *peace and calm*,
For respite and release from you.
You sit upon our conscience and our brain
Like black spiders in a knot ...
You say that we accuse you falsely,
And you scurry and you work to prove us liars.
You defend yourselves —
Why do you lack the courage to proclaim it
To the world, with dignity and pride,
And say: Yes, we do drink blood for Passover!

It's what binds our unleavened bread!
We've always drunk it, always will! *(Laughs at his own words.)*
We burn you at the stake, and though you're innocent,
You go as willingly to be burned as if invited to a ball!
Why don't you attack us
As we do you, with torch and axe?
And even now, this moment, as I speak,
Why don't you answer?
Where is there one among you with the courage
To step forward, seize my staff,
And break it on my skull. You say nothing!
All you do is wait for me to shout: Get out!
Always, always ready to depart —
So be it, then, go! GO! *GET OUT! (All the beggars jump up and run as if from a fire, exiting.)*
Such dogs. Give them a command, and they run. *(Listening.)*
Do you hear that? Steps?
Is one of them still left?
MONK.
No one's here, Father.
THADDEUS.
But don't you hear the steps?
MONK.
It's your fancy only.
THADDEUS.
Then hear me: Now that they're gone
This place — deserted and unknown —
Shall stay that way
For none of them will dare return.
And so it shall be a temple of quiet and privacy
For the deed that I have asked you to perform.
MONK.
Tell me again what I must do —
THADDEUS.
Again! Your fear and weakness
Show in this ability to forget!
MONK.
I'm sorry Father —

THADDEUS.
Then hear it now: To this place you'll come when the moon is new
And let your hands not tremble as you hold the knife
Firmly, in your left hand,
While you hold the throat of the child
In your right: Let not an outcry
Not a shudder pass through these walls.
Then I will come and help you finish the work.
MONK.
My head spins to listen, Father —
THADDEUS.
(Grabbing the Monk's garment by the neck.) Are you afraid?
Do you not see who leads you?
Do you not see my gray beard,
My staff of age
And in my eyes the nights I lie awake?
MONK.
I'm sorry, please forgive me —
THADDEUS.
(Letting go.) I do forgive you. So feel blessed — *(A thud is heard.)*
There: again!
MONK.
Now I hear it —
THADDEUS.
And there — *(Sound of louder, approaching thudding steps.)*
I *do* hear steps. What's going on?
I feel a movement in the air —
MONK.
My knees give way —
THADDEUS.
Holy Saviour, protect us! *(There is a whistling and a whirling in the air about them, as though someone were whipping long, wet rods about their heads. Steps of great, unseen feet are heard. The lights go out as though torches have been extinguished. Now only thin strips of moonlight streak the room. Terrible blows begin to descend on the heads of Thaddeus and the Monk. They dodge about in wild terror from the invisible attacker, duck down to the floor, run to the doors, but wherever they go the blows of unseen hands pursue them.)*

The place is haunted! Evil spirits! Run! *(But they are stopped at every door and thrown back. And the blows don't stop falling on their heads. Their noses begin to bleed. The sound of a snap is the breaking of Thaddeus' arm. He screams in pain, as he and the Monk finally escape out the door. Their footsteps recede in the distance, as light suddenly floods in from a second doorway. The Golem strides in, his face pale, his eyes aflame, gasping for breath. He leans against a wall, slumps to the floor.)*
GOLEM.
Where are you, Rabbi? Where are you?
MAHARAL. *(Hurrying in.)*
I'm here —
GOLEM.
(Getting to his knees, clutching at the Maharal.) Rabbi!
Don't leave me, take me by the hand —
MAHARAL.
(Taking the Golem's hand.) You've passed the test!
Glory will follow —
GOLEM.
It's dark, Rabbi, dark,
Don't go away.
MAHARAL.
You've done your work
With magnificence — now rest: sleep.
GOLEM.
Don't go. Don't go —
MAHARAL.
There's still much to do,
But not without sleep.
Lie down now. *(The Golem lies down on the hard floor, curls into a fetal position.)*
Go to sleep. *(The Maharal exits. The Golem lies there, alone. An inhuman sound of despairing loneliness issues from his throat. He twists and turns, but can't find comfort. The beginning of end-of-act music is heard.)*
GOLEM.
Oh, Rabbi, stay with me. *(He makes the same moan again.)*
Why is it quiet? *(Stretching out his arms in agony.)*
Why is it so dark...? *(A flourish of music — a plunge into darkness.)*

ACT TWO

Scene 5

A field outside of Prague. Night. Chunks of cloud in the sky.
The Old Beggar and the Young Beggar sit beside a road lead-
ing off into the distance.

YOUNG BEGGAR.
No one came to hear my summons
Or to greet me on the road that led to Prague.
Instead they all flocked in breathless fever
To see the Golem's wonder, not mine.
The Golem has become the savior,
With his fist and with his axe —
OLD BEGGAR.
There's no more that you or I can do
Except to sleep: sleep and rest —
God-defended, God-protected —
YOUNG BEGGAR.
Let us leave this place.
I see the smoke rising from the burning stakes:
And mine is not to help these victims —
But neither can I die with them.
OLD BEGGAR.
Where are these horrors you describe?
YOUNG BEGGAR.
You can't see them, or hear?
Stifled outcries coming towards us?
OLD BEGGAR.
Whose?

YOUNG BEGGAR.
Cries from far-off … *(Taking hold of the Old Beggar's sleeve.)*
Silence me then …
OLD BEGGAR.
Lie and rest:
Let your heart know consolation,
For yours is the journey
Chosen by almighty God.
YOUNG BEGGAR.
Take me back into the desert,
For I grow fearful in this stillness …
I see lopped off heads and limbs like stubble:
Eyes are bursting and running out;
Fire and flame, and all of this
While two men just sit here, studying the clock-hands
Slowly dragging — you and I.
All the throats have long been cut.
And yet the two of us just sit here, waiting …
And then we walk away. *(Clasps the knees of the Old Beggar.)*
Forgive me that I open wounds that can't be healed.
Forgive me that I bite
Bleeding lips to make them feel … *(He falls asleep. The Old Beggar
sits watching over him. The Maharal enters in a hurry — impatient,
but clearly at war with his own words:)*
MAHARAL.
Are you still here?
Must you be ordered more than once?
OLD BEGGAR.
Don't be angry —
MAHARAL.
Begone at once!
A single second is too long!
OLD BEGGAR.
The road is long and dark.
MAHARAL.
Don't speak to me of darkness. Let it suffice
That I choke back some weeping of my own,
That I restrain my knees from bending,

From falling down before him myself: Have pity.
Woe would be to me and woe to him
Were I to drive this hardness from my heart.
Why did you have to bring him here?
So that he could see the face of death and danger?
What can he do for us? What *should* he do?
The world has not yet exhausted
Its store of cruelty on us.
OLD BEGGAR.
Oh, Levi, Levi —
MAHARAL.
Take him away. Don't contaminate his heart with our dread.
Return when the violence is done.
How can we open our arms to greet him
On a road that's strewn with corpses?
Who among us will sing his praises:
The man whose throat's been cut in half?
He has to go —
Can his fingers coil into iron
And smash the skulls of our enemies?
Can he stand the smell of blood?
Can he spill it? Can he exact a tooth for a tooth
And an eye for an eye?
Can those gentle hands of his scratch in the filth?
No: And I would be the first to stand opposed
If *he* should *try* to help us,
With his peaceful methods, doomed to failure —
OLD BEGGAR.
He came to help:
His heart was full of longing for you.
MAHARAL.
Let him muffle that longing.
There's another who will do my bidding.
And he's the only one permitted to be dark,
Permitted to spill blood for blood.
For we, as yet, deserve no better to defend us.
OLD BEGGAR.
(To the Young Beggar.) Wake up. We must depart.

YOUNG BEGGAR.
(Waking, to the Maharal.) You come once more to drive us? *(Slowly getting to his feet.)*
Why don't you allow me this night's sleep?
MAHARAL.
This night will be a night of blood.
YOUNG BEGGAR.
My eyes are eager to observe such a night.
MAHARAL.
(His resolve weakening.) Let them rather be struck blind —
YOUNG BEGGAR.
My ears long to hear the cries for help —
MAHARAL.
(Struggling to believe his own words.)
Instead you should be stricken deaf —
YOUNG BEGGAR.
My lips are thirsting to recite
The Confession with the dying —
MAHARAL.
(Looking away.) Better for them to be mute.
YOUNG BEGGAR.
Have you no warmer words for me? *(The Maharal turns back to look at him, but doesn't reply. The Young Beggar reaches out and touches the Maharal's forehead. The Maharal, exhausted and conflicted, closes his eyes and bows his head.)*
Then I will take them as the speech of love. I came
Myself, awaiting no one's call.
I wanted to walk through the world,
And look into the eyes of men.
But those eyes were looking somewhere else:
My glances were left hanging in the air … *(The Maharal opens his eyes, which have begun to well up with tears, and raises his face — the Young Beggar removes his hand, looks down the road.)*
Now the only thing I want is rest.
Perhaps I came one moment late,
One stroke of time too soon.
Since it was I who chose to come,
How can the world be held accountable?

54

Is it obliged to stop its murders? *(Looks back at the Maharal.)*
In the desert I'll find the sleep I've lost ...
Joy to you and all of you. *(Exits with the Old Beggar.)*
MAHARAL.
(Impulsively reaching out after them, but remaining rooted to the spot.) Not with honor,
As should be,
Did we greet
Our guest — nor glee — *(Lowering his arm.)*
Not the comfort
Of a bed;
Not with water,
Not with bread — *(Begins to pace uneasily.)*
Not a rag
His wounds to bind.
Not a blessing:
Fate be kind — *(Turns to watch them.)*
On he hastens,
On he runs,
Back again
He must not come. *(Tears spring to his eyes again.)*
Neither young
Nor yet the old
Ever will
His face behold ... *(Lowering his head, he leans on his staff. Now he weeps ... The sky has become completely overcast. A strong wind begins to blow. A storm is brewing.)*
No more, no more,
Alas, no more ... *(His head bowed, the wind rips at his clothing.)*

Scene 6

In Tower Five. The Golem is lying face-down, asleep. The rain whips in through the windows. Tankhum, drenched by the rain, appears at the door. He does not yet notice the Golem.

TANKHUM.
(To himself.) Cowards!
I knocked at every door, and
Banged on every shutter, shouting:
"Prepare a welcome! He is here!"
But Prague is dead.
Without rhyme or reason
Prague is dead. *(Sound of thunder.)*
GOLEM.
(Mumbling in his sleep.) No more, no more … alas no more …
TANKHUM.
(Seeing the Golem.) He sleeps. But soon he'll awaken
And be a witness — *(Shouting at the Golem:)*
Who is no more? What is no more?
GOLEM.
(Awakens, slowly sits up.) He drove them both away.
Now he stands there and grieves
"No more, no more."
TANKHUM.
Then who will save us?
Tell me: *you?*
Who will save us? (The Golem leaps up suddenly, takes hold of Tankhum's arm.)
GOLEM.
Don't go away. Stay here —
TANKHUM.
(Shrinking from the strength of the grab, suddenly confused.)
I've forgotten who you are —

GOLEM.
You don't know me? I'll become another.
I'm condemned to suffer here.
I'm revolted by my own flesh,
By my staring, glassy eyes.
My days and nights grow dusty here;
While desire urges me to fly off into the distance —
TANKHUM.
(Now grabbing the Golem's arm in turn.) Then tell me who you are.
In Tower Five, the darkness has revealed its deepest secrets to me:
Are you one of those mysteries?
You've been given a sacred task
Haven't you? Tell me: Haven't you?
GOLEM.
I'm the secret, not of darkness, but of light,
And your gaping at me will discover nothing
Though you burst your eyes with staring.
TANKHUM.
(Now grabbing the Golem's shoulders and shaking him.) The task!
  Reveal it to me!
You'll give to *them* what they gave to my son!?
The gaping holes, the swinging limbs,
The blood that never stops flowing!?
GOLEM.
(In a suddenly stony voice, as a strange light begins to glow around him.) I warn you now: Don't look at me.
If you raise your eyes to me a second time,
You'll die.
TANKHUM.
(Weakening.) But I am everlasting —
GOLEM.
(Gripping Tankhum's hands and removing them from his shoulders.)
No: You can die.
I am the one who's everlasting —
TANKHUM.
(Suddenly fearful.) Then horror and catastrophe:
Death and calamity!
In piles the bodies will rise —

More victims, like my son,
And no one to protect them —
Who will save us!? *(From a remote part of the tower a woman's voice
is heard calling for "Help!" The call echoes through the ruins.)*
TANKHUM.
"Help" — who should help?
THE CALL.
(Again.) Help!
TANKHUM.
Who can help?
Who wants to help? Eh?
Who should help? *(Breaks into mad laughter, breaks free from the
Golem.)*
Who will save us!? Eh? Who!? *(As he runs out, we hear his cackling
receding.)*
Who will save us…? *(Exits. As approaching footsteps are heard, the
Golem moves into the shadows. Devorale and the Rebbetsin enter,
looking terrified, clinging to each other.)*
DEVORALE.
So many doors and caves; where do they lead?
REBBETSIN.
And who's to blame? You are. Such folly
To come here looking for your father!
What would he be doing in these ruins?
DEVORALE.
Now you scold me,
But you yourself said we should go —
REBBETSIN.
Yes — since midnight came and went
Without your father home
From evening prayers.
DEVORALE.
My hands are raw. The walls
Are full of nails —
REBBETSIN.
Let's look again.
Somewhere there's a door that leads outside —

DEVORALE.
Mother, I feel dizzy —
REBBETSIN.
Hold onto me, dear child — *(The Golem suddenly steps out of the shadows, the same eerie glow of light surrounding him. Both women let out a scream.)*
GOLEM.
Why are you afraid? I come
To save you and lead you out —
REBBETSIN.
Go away — leave us — !
GOLEM.
Who else will come to save you?
I alone.
DEVORALE.
(Less afraid than her mother.) You're … Joseph, are you not?
GOLEM.
Joseph is not my name today; there's
Another Joseph now, one who no longer
Lies on the floor, no longer
Sleeps in the darkness.
I knew the Rabbi would have kept me back,
And so I didn't ask for his permission.
Why do you look at me with such fear?
DEVORALE.
(Her voice calm, nonetheless.) Because … you frighten us.
GOLEM.
Then I'll have to make you unafraid.
You see, within my heart
A love awoke, a longing.
I'm impatient for the moment when
I can lie back down … *(Slowly he sits on the ground.)*
I'm weary. May I sit down?
REBBETSIN.
What is he asking us? What does he want?
GOLEM.
I won't harm you —
Why do you tremble so —

59

I'm becoming luminous,
Brighter than he, the young wanderer,
And brighter than the Rabbi. Should I tell
You where the young man's feet are treading now?
And where — the Rabbi's?
REBBETSIN.
Have you seen the Rabbi?
GOLEM.
Have I seen him? I see him always.
The steps of the wanderer disappear,
But the Rabbi comes. He's returning now.
REBBETSIN.
Where is he coming from?
GOLEM.
From the field beyond the city.
I saw the Rabbi standing there in sorrow,
His head bowed — while he, the wanderer,
Went plodding on, step by step ...
Oh, how much I longed to follow him,
To be with him,
To lie down at his feet and be his shadow ... *(Looking toward a doorway.)*
The Rabbi is coming.
He tarries, his steps are heavy
His head sinks beneath the weight of sorrow. *(Looking back at the women.)*
You would be blinded in a single instant
Were you to look at me against my will —
REBBETSIN.
Oh, God, we must escape —
GOLEM.
You're still afraid? Don't be: The Rabbi is near. *(Turning to Devorale:)*
You look into my eyes, and I recall the moment
When I pressed you close to me.
I can still feel your warmth on my fingers,
And at my breast I can still feel you trembling. *(The Rebbetsin protectively throws her arms around Devorale, trying to shield her from*

the Golem's words.)
Then I couldn't speak; I couldn't catch my breath. It's different now.
I don't even want to touch you.
It's enough for me to sit, face to face with you, as I sit now, and
speak ...
If I should wish, I could grab you and hurl you in the air
And spin you round my head so long and fast
That your hands would grapple round my neck
And your lips, aflame with hurt, locked in pain,
Would suck themselves into my own — *(He stands up. The
Rebbetsin faints into her daughter's lap. Devorale continues staring up
at the Golem, not taking her eyes off his.)*
Come, let me lead you out. I'm revolted
By your fear and still more by my revelation
Of myself. I'm shamed enough
That I couldn't pass you by
Without remembering your warmth on my fingers,
That I revealed to you so many secrets;
Come: I'll lead the way. *(He touches the Rebbetsin's shoulder. She
awakens as if in a trance.)*
I'll show the way for you to leave.
Follow me. *(He takes them by the hands and helps them stand up.
Both women, now, seem to be in a trance as they follow him.)*
You needn't fear because I touch you.
I only lead you, I only show the way. *(He leads them out. At the sec-
ondary exit (not the one all of them used to enter), he appears to "steer"
them on their way.)*
On the right, stay on the right:
Follow to the right — *(He gazes after their departure; then turns
back to the room.)*
The Rabbi now comes this way,
Like me, to seek the warmth of these four walls,
Where he's always certain to find one — me —
Who waits for him ... *(He lies on the ground in the same prone posi-
tion as at the scene's beginning. The Maharal enters carrying a lantern.)*
MAHARAL.
(Illuminating the Golem with his lantern.) Get up. It's time. Get up.

GOLEM.
(Rising.) Rabbi —
MAHARAL.
(Rapidly.) There never was less time today
Nor more tomorrow.
It is, in fact, *your* time — *our* time —
And to that end I summon you —
GOLEM.
I'm ready, Rabbi —
MAHARAL.
Those powers that gave you life
Will also give you knowledge and let you
See through walls and floors and into the hearts
Of those that would destroy us.
Therefore watch the godless men and
Protect us from them. Go now:
Catch those who would plant a lifeless body,
A vial of blood — who would cause such lies
To be made manifest and written
Where they cannot be erased.
GOLEM.
I will obey, Rabbi,
But how long shall I live?
MAHARAL.
(Stunned by this last remark.) Live?
GOLEM.
Yes, Rabbi, how long shall I live?
MAHARAL.
(After a pause — then vehemently, almost shaking:)
Until the Jews are no longer in danger,
That is when — at my command —
And not before, Joseph,
You will return to the earth from
Whence you came.
Do you understand? *(The Golem is silent.)*
You do not understand — ?
GOLEM.
(After pause.) I will obey you, Rabbi.

MAHARAL.
Good. As well, my wife and daughter
Have been missing since the *Maariv* —
Six hours now — so tell me: Can you
Use your powers to find them too,
And bring them home?
GOLEM.
(Looking out, and off: seeing a vision.)
They're home now, Rabbi —
They are safe.
MAHARAL.
Safe? *(Relieved; now warmer to the Golem.)*
You're part of the earth,
And the earth knows many things — *(Taking hold of the Golem's shoulder.)*
Now hear the word that I reveal to you
And grasp it well. See its redness;
Perceive its warmth and its sharpness.
The word is — blood.
GOLEM.
Blood.
MAHARAL.
Repeat again —
GOLEM.
Blood.
MAHARAL.
Again but softer.
GOLEM.
Blood.
MAHARAL.
Come — *(They both exit out the main doorway. After a second, Tankhum enters from the secondary doorway: Clearly he has just been eavesdropping, hearing everything. He holds a candle and glides across the stage, pursuing the Rabbi and the Golem, but addressing the audience, face on:)*
TANKHUM.
(In a strained voice.) Who will save us? Eh?
Who will save us? *(As he exits:)*

Who will save us — ? *(His voice fading.)*
Who will save us … ?

Scene 7

In the anteroom of the Synagogue. Thaddeus, using a crutch, and wearing a white robe — and with his arm in some kind of a sling — hobbles closer to the Monk, who is kneeling on the floor. Thaddeus holds a torch aloft, illuminating what the Monk is doing: sharpening a blade on a stone. A swaddled bundle is on the ground, next to an empty sack and several empty glass vials. The eerie chanting that accompanied Thaddeus in the past is heard faintly again.

THADDEUS.
Steady now. It should be sharp enough.
MONK.
(Nervously.) The infant is still asleep, Father —
THADDEUS.
Then you will do it now, before it wakes —
MONK.
(Wringing his hands.) But why must it be *here*?
Why in the synagogue?
There's no more dangerous place if the child should scream —
THADDEUS.
Then lead the way back to Tower Five: I will follow you.
I still have one good limb left for them to break in half!
You seek another visit from the devils
That set themselves upon us!?
No I say — *here* we'll do the deed.
Here is where it belongs:
Where the worshipping is done. *(The Monk's hand, holding the knife, trembles uncontrollably.)*

MONK.

Forgive me, Father, I can't stop this shaking —

In my heart as well —

THADDEUS.

(Furiously.) This mission was ordained for us by God himself!

Do not hesitate — *(The Monk lifts the swaddled bundle, cradling it in his left arm. The chanting is heard loudly now. Slowly he raises the knife in his right hand, which trembles wildly: He can't seem to bring the blade down on the baby's throat … Just at that moment, the baby wakes with a cry.)*

Now, damn you, *now* — ! *(The Monk is on the verge of dropping the bundle and the knife in terror … When suddenly Thaddeus snatches the knife from the Monk and — in one fluid motion — draws the blade across the baby's throat. The baby's crying is aborted. Thaddeus lets his crutch fall onto the ground, but keeps a tight hold on the blood-stained knife.)*

Now fill the vials — and tell me:

For whose sake do we work at night? Our own? No … *(The Monk takes one empty vial after another, and — as Thaddeus talks — fills them with blood coming from inside the swaddled bundle. The Monk wears a terrified expression throughout these actions, as he listens to Thaddeus:)*

Watching you work

I'm more than calm. I'm exultant.

I see before my eyes such visions

As no one but He could have seen

While He still hung, nailed to the cross —

And He must have seen the same visions that I behold now:

This knife too. Glittering, gleaming,

Caressing His open lid;

You think to yourself: "sabotage"? No. Love alone.

For blood is — love. Blood of children,

Since He was also a child. And every knife

From that time on has been blessed.

For there must never be an end to the flowing,

Of the blood of those who cannot see

The gentle gleam His closing eyelid cast …

MONK.

(Setting the last full bottle down.) Father, someone comes, I think —

THADDEUS.

You have fears of every kind. Coward! Who would come here?

(As the Monk puts the baby's swaddled corpse into the sack:)

You hear the sound of steps? Of course. Those steps are His.

Softly, lovingly he hovers over us

And breathes in deep the crimson scent.

Yes: He's here with us as well. He comes!

His pale cheeks flush,

And from His eyes the joy of love flows,

And childlike tenderness and pity.

He bears the cross upon His shoulders. He dances with it;

He sings with it,

He is here — Jesus Christ, our Lord!

Do you not see Him? Raise your eyes!

MONK.

(Crossing himself in terror.) I'm afraid of your words — !
   Blasphemy — !

THADDEUS.

What: You can't see!?

MONK.

Oh, merciful Jesus, have pity!

Holy Father, take me from this place!

THADDEUS.

Run away then!

You're deaf and blind if you can't see! Away!

(The Monk jumps up in terror and runs — but just as he reaches the exit, his way is blocked by the Golem, who carries his axe. The Golem grabs the Monk and tosses him aside; then fixes his gaze on Thaddeus. The chanting that we've heard throughout has by now reached its peak volume. The Golem takes two steps toward Thaddeus, who takes two limping steps backwards, but continues holding the knife out in front of himself protectively. The Golem suddenly looks down at the floor and — seeing the sack and the vials there — instinctively walks over to them. He drops the axe on the floor, picks up the sack and, opening it, begins putting the corked vials inside. Suddenly, with a cry, Thaddeus runs at the Golem and stabs the knife into his back, but it doesn't penetrate the

skin. The Golem spins round to face Thaddeus, who has now picked up his crutch, and swings it once, twice, trying to strike the Golem's face. The Golem grabs the crutch with one hand, hurls it aside, then grabs Thaddeus with both hands about the throat. Thaddeus, the knife still in his hand, stabs at the Golem repeatedly.

The Golem seizes Thaddeus' wrist and slowly, steadily, turns the knife back towards Thaddeus, finally plunging it into Thaddeus' heart. Thaddeus goes limp all at once. The Golem lets go of him, as he slides dead onto the floor. The Golem then turns, sees the Monk cringing in terror near the entrance. In a flash the Monk is on his feet and — screaming "Help me God!!" — he runs out, exiting. The Golem grabs the sack and his axe off the floor and gives chase. The music shifts to a full orchestral pound. Blackout.)

Scene 8

The Monk enters on the run, stops in the glare of the moonlight — in the town square perhaps — and shouts to all, in an attempt to wake the town:

MONK.
Wake up! Wake up!
A giant has killed Thaddeus in the synagogue!
They'll kill us all! Wake up! *(Bells begin to clang, as The Monk is joined by a Crowd of shouting townsfolk, who rush onstage carrying torches and pickaxes. Glass smashing is heard as well as screams of "Kill the Jews!", "Kill them all!", "Christ bleeds!", "The Jews have desecrated the Host!", etc. Sounds of looting accompany the crowd as they sweep off the stage ...*

Enter the Golem, still carrying the sack and his axe. He sits on the ground in a pool of moonlight, stares blankly down at his lap, as the sound of the pogrom continues to rage around him. Enter the Maharal on the run.)

MAHARAL.

Great God, why are you sitting here?

Your people need you, can't you hear? *(Sees the sack, picks it up.)*

One deed is done — quickly, now, remove it! *(Throws the sack in the Golem's lap.)*

Arise! Get up! Why do you sit!? *(The Golem doesn't move his head, says nothing.)*

Do you not see who speaks to you!? *(Shakes him by the shoulders.)*

I tell you, speak!

GOLEM.

(Looks at the Maharal — lowers his head again.)

Who are you? Go away.

MAHARAL.

You don't know me?

GOLEM.

I do not.

MAHARAL.

(Shaking him by the shoulders again.) What's happened to you?

Your entire life is but an expectation

Of those moments when I need you!

And now one has come, you still don't perceive

How great your destiny is, how

The accidental and the superfluous

Of your life depart! Deeds and prowess call!

Grace descends upon you, and over you

The protecting wings of Providence unfold!

GOLEM.

(Pulling his shoes off one-by-one; wearing an expression of despair.)

Let me be! Remove this blood — ! *(Angrily hurling the shoes and sack away.)*

Remove it! Take it far away!

MAHARAL.

(Grabbing the Golem's head.) Be calm and look at me.

Be yourself again.

GOLEM.

Who are you? You wish to sit?

It's forbidden.

This spot is marked and bounded

68

For me alone and no one else.

MAHARAL.

(Rising wrathfully.) Let this madness leave you!
Your mission still is not fulfilled —
The danger grows with every second:
Who are *you* that for your sake
The redemption of a people
Should be delayed for even half an instant!
Awaken! If your eyes are blinded,
Then seek with blinded eyes; but bring back
The brightness that I gave you!

GOLEM.

The brightness that you take with you when you leave —

MAHARAL.

(Helping the Golem to his feet.) Come, go to it. Say the words:
"Through death and blood."
Begin the journey and say with me:
"Through death and blood — "

GOLEM.

(Rising.) "Through death and blood — "

MAHARAL.

(Leading the Golem downstage, handing him the axe.)
You must go alone.
You need no torch, but take the axe!
Your stride is long; your eye is bright —

GOLEM.

Come with me —

MAHARAL.

I mustn't.
With a thousand eyes, peril seeks a pretext.
I bid you go alone.
"Through death and blood — "

GOLEM.

"Through death and blood — "

MAHARAL.

(Exiting.) "Your stride is long — "

GOLEM.

"Through death and blood — "

MAHARAL.

(His voice fading as he exits "Through death and blood — " *(The Golem now stands alone, downstage, facing out, holding the axe. The sound of the Pogrom is overpoweringly loud. The Golem turns his back to us, and — silhouetted — raises the axe up, holding it aloft for a moment. ... Then down it swings, then up, then down, in slow, fluid motions, accompanied by a montage of sound: the shouts of frightened fleeing men, of footsteps, of the groans of the wounded and the dying, of the final dispersal of the Crowd. The impression should be that the Golem is single-handedly stopping the riotous pogrom ... The violent flames from torches seem to gradually be going out, and in their place the cooler light of lamps appears. ...*

These lamps come onstage: It is now a procession, heading toward the synagogue. Joyous, talis-covered Jews surround the Golem — they clutch at him in gratitude. All are in a state of exultation.)

ISAAC.

(To Jacob.) Did you not hear about the miracle?

JACOB.

Thanks be to God — the pogrom was stopped!

ISAAC.

With his mighty hands, the woodcutter brought them to their knees!

REB BASSEVI.

(Clapping the Golem on the back.)

With his great strength he doused the flames —

JEW #1.

Our homes were saved!

JEW #2.

By a Golem!

ISAAC.

A man of might — !

REB BASSEVI.

A people's champion — !

JACOB.

(Dissentingly.) A thing of clay —

REB BASSEVI.

No: a living man!

JEW #3.

(Looking out from inside the door of the synagogue.)

70

The Rabbi has arrived.
The service will begin — *(All continue talking excitedly as they head into the synagogue:)*
JEW #2.
But greater still:
While the Emperor's soldiers gathered round
The Monk — held by the throat —
Confessed that Thaddeus had killed the child!
ISAAC.
Before the crowd he called him "Satan,"
And begged for mercy
As he threw himself upon the ground!
REB BASSEVI.
A miracle —
JEW #1.
On the eve of Passover —
JEW #2.
The Jews are saved —
REB BASSEVI.
Thanks be to God! *(The last of them files into the synagogue, leaving the Golem alone on the street ...*

At that moment, Tankhum dashes in, eyes bulging, his body drenched in sweat. He stops dead in his tracks when he sees the Golem.)
TANKHUM.
(To the Golem.) Do you remember: the Young One and the Old —
The ones you scared away?
Who will save us!? Is it you!? *(The Golem just stares at him.)*
You silent lump: Answer me!
Who will save us!? *(The Golem continues staring, uncomprehending. Tankhum rushes at him, grabs the axe.)*
Is this salvation!? This!? *(They wrestle with the axe, the Golem barely expending an ounce of energy to hold onto it. Tankhum twists and turns, trying to wrest the axe from the Golem. Finally, he bites the Golem's hand to get him to let go. The Golem unconsciously jerks his arm upwards in surprise, then — suddenly angry and narrowing his eyes — he advances on Tankhum, holding the axe aloft with both hands, threatening. Tankhum shrieks, cowers on the ground, holds up his hands in defense — when suddenly Devorale enters, alone.)*

71

DEVORALE.
(Shouting, terrified.) Stop! I beg you! *(The Golem whips around at the sound of her voice, stares at her in wonder.)*
Put it down — *(The Golem slowly lowers the axe.)*
You should be ashamed — *(The axe drops from the Golem's hands. Tankhum scurries off, exits.)*
Why would you hurt him?
GOLEM.
I didn't think I would hurt him.
DEVORALE.
I saw you raise the axe.
GOLEM.
Yes. But I won't hurt him. Not now ... *(Taking a step toward her.)*
I have never seen you alone.
You are always with your mother —
DEVORALE.
Yes ... *(A small wave of fear passes through her — which she conquers — then, raising her chin, she takes a step herself toward the Golem.)*
She went out looking to find my father
In this night, so full of fire and bloodshed —
GOLEM.
Bloodshed —
DEVORALE.
They're calling you a hero,
A people's champion.
GOLEM.
But I don't want to be a hero:
That's what comes from shedding blood ...
(Looks down.) I want to be a man, an ordinary soul —
DEVORALE.
(Taking another step toward him, gently.) What makes you think you're
Not an ordinary soul?
GOLEM.
(Hopefully.) You think that I might be? *(Joy floods the Golem's heart; he goes right up to Devorale, touches her arm.)*
No sooner do I see you than
I'm afraid to blink
In case you disappear again —

DEVORALE.

I'm not leaving now.

GOLEM.

You're not — ? *(Tears fill his eyes.)*

And you will not leave again — ?

DEVORALE.

(Moved, touches his cheek.) How did you come by so much longing?

How did such an emptiness fill your soul?

It's as though no mother's breath

In childhood hovered over you —

No angel's wing brushed your crib —

GOLEM.

(Taking her hand in his.) No: no mother, and no father —

No people, and no faith. *(Drawing her closer.)*

Just a mission. And a task.

And endless isolation —

DEVORALE.

(Letting herself be held.) The Lord will comfort your soul with

The rescue of your people — and His.

GOLEM.

How sweet is the aroma of your hair.

How warm your hands.

DEVORALE.

Your hands are cold, Joseph —

GOLEM.

I hold you firmly. You are mine.

You came to me.

DEVORALE.

(Uncomfortably.) And I will come to you again,

But for now perhaps I —

GOLEM.

(Beginning to hug her.) In the tower above us, day and night I lay

Waiting for you to come and stay with me.

I thought that every rustle was a herald of your coming —

DEVORALE.

(Squirming a bit.) And so to you I will come again, but —

GOLEM.

(Rapturously.) Don't forsake me, I beg you —

I could toss you on my shoulders now,
And carry you back to the tower —
DEVORALE.
(Struggling to be released.) I beg you, please,
Don't hold me in this way —
GOLEM.
(Oblivious to her discomfort.) And we could twine together into one
And huddle in the covering of emptiness.
And I would open my eyes and see
The wind shredding your garments into tatters,
The lightning laying bare the whiteness of your skin,
The emptiness overflowing with your warmth:
And I would bite into your limbs
And suck your white flesh into myself —
DEVORALE.
(Now striking his shoulder.) No — stop it —
Don't speak to me this way — !
GOLEM.
(Not hearing her.) All is spinning once again, you see,
And now I'm well, and all is bright — *(Devorale uses all her strength
to get away, but the Golem simply sways with her struggle, and —
now lifting her face to his — tries to kiss her.)*
My well of breath runs dry —
DEVORALE.
(Jerking her head this way and that.) No — ! No — !
GOLEM.
I want your nearness, Devorale,
Just your nearness —
If only for this moment … *(The Golem holds her tight and achieves
his goal of kissing her. She continues to struggle, but her movements are
now less pronounced: He's holding her too tight, unknowingly preventing
her from breathing. In his grasp, she's now lifted off the ground. And
we can see by the decreased movement of her dangling arms and legs
that she is accidentally being suffocated. When the kiss is finished, she
goes limp in his arms: She is dead. The Golem doesn't absorb this fact,
until — letting her go — she slides lifelessly to the ground.*

*He's stunned for a moment and stands as still as a statue — staring
down at her … Finally, he bends down, scoops her up in his arms. He's*

trembling all over and begins to weep with the realization of what he's done. Carrying her now, he plods with heavy steps, heading off into the distance (towards the exit), convulsed with sobbing:)
Back to our tower we shall go —
You came to me, I was afraid to blink — *(A sob chokes his throat.)*
An ordinary soul — *(He stops.)*
A thing of clay — *(He raises his face to the sky, lets out an ungodly howl; then shouts at the top of his lungs:)*
Darkness! Conceal me again! *(Music strikes on a blackout.)*

Scene 9

Outside the Synagogue, a short while later: The dramatic transitional music continues, underscoring as the lights come up on the Golem — barefoot, alone — pounding on the doors of the synagogue, with the axe still in his hands — loudly, repeatedly — all the while bellowing:

GOLEM.
Bring me the Rabbi!! I want the Rabbi!! *(The door is finally flung open by Reb Bassevi: The sound of prayers comes flooding out from behind him.)*
REB BASSEVI.
Why such an outcry —
What do you want?
GOLEM.
Bring me the Rabbi!
REB BASSEVI.
(Noticing the Golem's bare feet.) It's forbidden to walk barefoot
In synagogue — *(The Golem doesn't reply.)*
Can't you hear them?
The prayers are already underway —
GOLEM.
I don't know how to pray!

Bring the Rabbi out here to *me* then ... ! *(Becoming enraged.)*
Tell him to bring me my shoes — !
REB BASSEVI.
Your shoes? The Rabbi?
GOLEM.
(Jumping up, screaming.) Tell him that I want him! That Joseph
wants him!
REB BASSEVI.
(Stopping the Golem with his hand.) Such impudence!
I've never heard the — ! *(The Golem violently shoves Reb Bassevi
aside, then smashes the glass of the synagogue door with his axe. He
kicks down the door and rushes inside. Though terrified, Reb Bassevi
runs in after the Golem.)*
Stop! Stop — !! *(Reb Bassevi exits into the synagogue, and immediately
we hear the shouts of panicking people, of benches being knocked over, of
stampeding feet, and of an axe striking — and finding — wood and
flesh. Screams are heard, as well as the groans of the wounded. The doors
of the synagogue burst open — Worshippers come pouring out, holding
their bleeding heads, limping, or being helped as they hobble outside.)*
JEW #1.
(Leaning on Isaac.) The woodcutter — !
JEW #2.
He'll kill us all —
JACOB.
(Helping Jew #3) Two are dead already —
REB BASSEVI.
A catastrophe —
JEW #3.
(Turning to look back.) The Rabbi's still inside —
ISAAC.
Let's go back —
JEW #2.
(Turning back as well.) We can't abandon them —
REB BASSEVI.
— A catastrophe for us! *(Suddenly the Maharal's voice roars above
the din:)*
MAHARAL.
(Furiously, from offstage.) — Betraying me, betraying us,

You *wretch* — !

Go! GO! GET OUT! *(The blood-spattered Golem suddenly bursts through the doors, his collar tightly held in the grip of the enraged and equally blood-spattered Maharal. The Golem is completely docile as the Maharal — holding the bloody axe in his other hand — literally pulls and drags the Golem by the neck out into the middle of the street, where — surrounded by the Crowd — he forces the Golem down onto his knees before him.)*

MAHARAL.

(White-faced and shaking with rage.) What were you told!?
What was your command!?
To turn on your own people!?
To turn on *me!?*
And for *this* did God call on us
To breathe the breath of life into you!?

GOLEM.

(Completely passive in the Maharal's grip.) I did not want it —

MAHARAL.

Want it!? Was this your choice!?
A people cried out
To be saved from the sword!
You worm, you lump of earth, you pile of dust — !! *(Turning to the Crowd:)*
Those who can, go back inside and
Tend to those who bleed —
Reb Bassevi —

REB BASSEVI.

Yes Rabbi —

MAHARAL.

(Gripping the Golem tighter.) How many are dead?

REB BASSEVI.

I think two … or maybe one, but I —

MAHARAL.

Save the ones who are still alive —
Isaac, Jacob — ! *(Reb Bassevi goes back into the synagogue, while Jew #2 helps #1 and #3 hobble off, exiting.)*

ISAAC and JACOB.

(Running up.) Yes Rabbi — !

MAHARAL.
Come down here into the light
And help me! *(The Maharal now forces the Golem to lie down on his back. As Isaac and Jacob come up alongside the Maharal, we hear the moans of the wounded still coming from inside the synagogue. The Maharal, Isaac and Jacob are now alone with the Golem.)*
MAHARAL.
(To Isaac and Jacob.) Both of you, take hold his shoulders — *(The Golem lies there without moving, silent tears streaming down his cheeks. Isaac and Jacob — unnecessarily — hold him down firmly by the shoulders.)*
GOLEM.
(In a hoarse whisper.) Do not forsake me —
MAHARAL.
(Closing his eyes.) On my head falls this blood. On my head — *(To the Golem, still shaken, but somewhat calmer:)*
What have you done? Does your mind grasp that? Tell me —
GOLEM.
I have spilled blood.
MAHARAL.
Whose blood was it you spilled?
GOLEM.
Jewish blood.
MAHARAL.
(Looking up at the sky, in deep anguish.) Are we thus chastised because
We wished to save ourselves oh Lord?
Did you allow me to create and command
Only that I might see my insignificance and my sin?
That in impatience and despair, I wished
To turn my back on the ways of our people —
So eternal, so gentle, so full of grace — *(Looking down at the Golem.)*
And for *this* I sent Him from us,
Made Him leave us, made Him go —
I refused Your faith and Your commandment that
We must wait and suffer and endure,
And still have faith in Your providence and mercy! *(Laying his palm on the Golem's forehead.)*
And now it's too late for me to bend my head

78

And let his axe taste my blood as well.
How great and just is Your chastisement, Lord —
GOLEM.
Now you will stay with me —
MAHARAL.
(Stroking the Golem's forehead, soothingly:) Yes —
The prisoner of your large fists —
GOLEM.
You will stay with me.
MAHARAL.
In a net of blood and muddied madness
I will stay here just with you ...
The candles will soon burn their last
And it will be dark — so unlike the Sabbath.
GOLEM.
The Rabbi will remain with me. *(Seeing a vision, he tries to rise.)*
You have come too? You will stay with me too, Devorale?
ISAAC.
What is he saying, Rabbi?
GOLEM.
(In a delirium.) How warm are your hands — *(Agitatedly.)*
Why do you run from me — !?
MAHARAL.
Rest now Joseph — *(Pulling out a gold handkerchief.)*
It's time to fulfill your last mission —
GOLEM.
(Slowly lying down.) Have I not performed every task, Rabbi?
MAHARAL.
Not the final one, Joseph.
You see, the candles are dying down.
A single light, the last, still flickers.
Soon it too will die —
GOLEM.
I'm afraid —
MAHARAL.
(Beginning to rub the Golem's forehead with the handkerchief.)
Here, before my eyes, you'll rest.
It's the Sabbath

And the earth, too, needs rest.

JACOB.

(To Isaac.) He erases the first letter —

GOLEM.

What will you do with me?

MAHARAL.

Listen to my words: I give you Sabbath rest.
Your whole life cries out for rest. *(Intoning:)*
Not of your will were you born,
And not of your will shall you die — *(A gust of wind kicks up.)*
I give you back to peace and darkness
And then to the light
That is the very presence of God — *(Lights and shadows flash and swirl across the sky — thunder is heard in the distance.)*

ISAAC.

(Clutching Jacob's arm, pointing at the Golem's forehead.)
You see: Now the word spells death —

GOLEM.

(Gulping at the air, convulsing.) Help me father —

MAHARAL.

(Ceases rubbing, suddenly lifting both his arms up high.) Into thy
     hand I commit this spirit!
Thou wilt surely redeem him, Oh Lord — *(A violent thunder-and-lightning flash.)*
Your dead shall live again —
But the mortal being shall return unto its rest! *(A final thunder clap, then quiet rolling thunder.)*

GOLEM.

(A whisper.) Do not ... forsake me ... *(The Golem dies. Isaac and Jacob remove their hands from the Golem's shoulders and — like the Maharal — sit there motionless, staring down at the dead body. All three are seated facing out. Behind them, the hint of dawn's breaking is seen.)*

MAHARAL.

(Quietly.) Isaac —

ISAAC.

Yes Rabbi? *(The Maharal inhales and exhales slowly with a sigh.)*

MAHARAL.
You will say the *Kaddish* —
JACOB.
(Delicately, not wanting to defy his mentor.) But … *can*
We say the sacred words Rabbi? That is … *(The Maharal looks up,
stares at Jacob.)*
… Can we let ourselves think of it as dead?
ISAAC.
"It"…? You mean "he" —
JACOB.
(To Isaac.) No: not "he." Not man. Not a living soul was this —
*(The Maharal gently raises his hand — which immediately quiets his
students.)*
MAHARAL.
Not a living soul? Perhaps …
Death and murder were his birthright:
And now — sadly, terribly — they are ours …
As Abraham built an altar to offer up his son,
So we shall have to build
A thousand altars before we're done.
*(The Maharal is quiet for another moment … then slowly he takes
hold of one edge of his vest, and* rips *the fabric in the area over his
heart: the sign of mourning … He then takes Isaac's and Jacob's hands
in his own, bows his head, and holds it there in silence for a while …
After pause:)*
    Yis'ga'dal v'yis'kadash sh'may ra'bbo,
    B'olmo dee'vro chir'usay v'yamlich malchu'say —
*(Isaac and Jacob close their eyes and now bow their heads as well,
intoning the Kaddish along with the Maharal. Their voices are qui-
eter than the voice of the rabbi, who leads. Even so, the Maharal
mumbles the prayer rapidly and quietly, the result of familiarity.)*
    B'chayaychon uv'yomay'chon uv'chayay d'chol bais Yisroel —
*(The lights slowly begin to fade — giving the impression that this is
the end of the play.)*
    Ba'agolo u'viz'man koriv; v'imru Omein.
    Y'hay shmay rabbo m'vorach
    L'olam ul'olmay olmayo. Yisborach —
(As the Maharal begins the last verse, the exhausted, breathless

Tankhum suddenly bursts onto the stage, coming to a running, stumbling halt — carrying the dead Devorale in his arms.)
TANKHUM.
(Shouting in horrified anguish at the backs of the three men:)
Who will save us!? *(The three men slowly turn to look, but before they can see the awful sight, we blackout.)*

End of Play

PROPERTY LIST

Tall, cross-shaped staff (THADDEUS)
Bundle (ISAAC)
Bread, pitcher of water, bowl (REBBETSIN)
Towel (REBBETSIN)
Axe (GOLEM, MAHARAL)
Bundles, torn pillows (SICK MAN, BEGGARS)
Little bags of coins (BLIND MAN, HUNCHBACK)
Bags and staffs (OLD BEGGAR, YOUNG BEGGAR)
Lantern (MAHARAL)
Candle (TANKHUM)
Crutch, arm-sling, torch (THADDEUS)
Knife-blade, sharpening stone, glass vials, swaddled bundle
(MONK)
Sack (MONK, GOLEM)
Blood (MONK)
Blood-filled vials (MONK)
Torches, pick-axes (CROWD)
Shoes (GOLEM)
Lanterns (CROWD)
Gold handkerchief (MAHARAL)

SOUND EFFECTS

Windows rattling
Walls shaking
Eerie chanting music
Approaching footsteps (thuds)
Whistling, whirring air
Blows
Snap of arm breaking
Wind
Thunder
Rain and wind
Baby crying
Church bells
Glass smashing, looting, pogrom
Sound montage: shouts, footsteps, groans
Prayers
Benches falling, axe hitting wood and flesh, screams, groans

NEW PLAYS

★ **SHEL'S SHORTS by Shel Silverstein.** Lauded poet, songwriter and author of children's books, the incomparable Shel Silverstein's short plays are deeply infused with the same wicked sense of humor that made him famous. "...[a] childlike honesty and twisted sense of humor." –*Boston Herald.* "...terse dialogue and an absurdity laced with a tang of dread give [*Shel's Shorts*] more than a trace of Samuel Beckett's comic existentialism." –*Boston Phoenix.* [flexible casting] ISBN: 0-8222-1897-6

★ **AN ADULT EVENING OF SHEL SILVERSTEIN by Shel Silverstein.** Welcome to the darkly comic world of Shel Silverstein, a world where nothing is as it seems and where the most innocent conversation can turn menacing in an instant. These ten imaginative plays vary widely in content, but the style is unmistakable. "...[*An Adult Evening*] shows off Silverstein's virtuosic gift for wordplay...[and] sends the audience out...with a clear appreciation of human nature as perverse and laughable." –*NY Times.* [flexible casting] ISBN: 0-8222-1873-9

★ **WHERE'S MY MONEY? by John Patrick Shanley.** A caustic and sardonic vivisection of the institution of marriage, laced with the author's inimitable razor-sharp wit. "...Shanley's gift for acid-laced one-liners and emotionally tumescent exchanges is certainly potent..." –*Variety.* "...lively, smart, occasionally scary and rich in reverse wisdom." –*NY Times.* [3M, 3W] ISBN: 0-8222-1865-8

★ **A FEW STOUT INDIVIDUALS by John Guare.** A wonderfully screwy comedy-drama that figures Ulysses S. Grant in the throes of writing his memoirs, surrounded by a cast of fantastical characters, including the Emperor and Empress of Japan, the opera star Adelina Patti and Mark Twain. "Guare's smarts, passion and creativity skyrocket to awesome heights..." –*Star Ledger.* "...precisely the kind of good new play that you might call an everyday miracle...every minute of it is fresh and newly alive..." –*Village Voice.* [10M, 3W] ISBN: 0-8222-1907-7

★ **BREATH, BOOM by Kia Corthron.** A look at fourteen years in the life of Prix, a Bronx native, from her ruthless girl-gang leadership at sixteen through her coming to maturity at thirty. "...vivid world, believable and eye-opening, a place worthy of a dramatic visit, where no one would want to live but many have to." –*NY Times.* "...rich with humor, terse vernacular strength and gritty detail..." –*Variety.* [1M, 9W] ISBN: 0-8222-1849-6

★ **THE LATE HENRY MOSS by Sam Shepard.** Two antagonistic brothers, Ray and Earl, are brought together after their father, Henry Moss, is found dead in his seedy New Mexico home in this classic Shepard tale. "...His singular gift has been for building mysteries out of the ordinary ingredients of American family life..." –*NY Times.* "...rich moments ...Shepard finds gold." –*LA Times.* [7M, 1W] ISBN: 0-8222-1858-5

★ **THE CARPETBAGGER'S CHILDREN by Horton Foote.** One family's history spanning from the Civil War to WWII is recounted by three sisters in evocative, intertwining monologues. "...bittersweet music—[a] rhapsody of ambivalence...in its modest, garrulous way...theatrically daring." –*The New Yorker.* [3W] ISBN: 0-8222-1843-7

★ **THE NINA VARIATIONS by Steven Dietz.** In this funny, fierce and heartbreaking homage to *The Seagull,* Dietz puts Chekhov's star-crossed lovers in a room and doesn't let them out. "A perfect little jewel of a play..." –*Shepherdstown Chronicle.* "...a delightful revelation of a writer at play; and also an odd, haunting, moving theater piece of lingering beauty." –*Eastside Journal (Seattle).* [1M, 1W (flexible casting)] ISBN: 0-8222-1891-7

DRAMATISTS PLAY SERVICE, INC.
440 Park Avenue South, New York, NY 10016 212-683-8960 Fax 212-213-1539
postmaster@dramatists.com www.dramatists.com

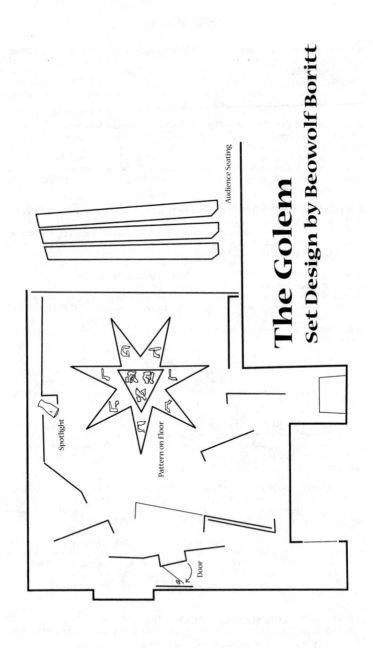

The Golem
Set Design by Beowolf Boritt

Audience Seating

Spotlight

Pattern on Floor

Door